Modular Matrix
A sample of modules from buildings in this book

THE MODULAR HOUSING HANDBOOK

SIMON BAYLISS & RORY BERGIN

RIBA Publishing

© RIBA Publishing, 2020

Published by RIBA Publishing, 66 Portland Place, London, W1B 1AD

ISBN 9781 85946 865 4

The rights of Simon Bayliss and Rory Bergin to be identified as the Authors of this Work have been asserted in accordance with the Copyright, Designs and Patents Act 1988 sections 77 and 78.

All rights reserved. No part of this publication may be reproduced, stored in a retrieval system, or transmitted, in any form or by any means, electronic, mechanical, photocopying, recording or otherwise, without prior permission of the copyright owner.

British Library Cataloguing-in-Publication Data
A catalogue record for this book is available from the British Library.

Commissioning Editor: Ginny Mills
Assistant Editor: Clare Holloway
Production: Sarah-Louise Deazley
Designed by Kneath Associates
Typeset by Alex Lazarou
Printed and bound by Short Run Press Limited, Exeter
Cover image: Peter Landers Photography

While every effort has been made to check the accuracy and quality of the information given in this publication, neither the Author nor the Publisher accept any responsibility for the subsequent use of this information, for any errors or omissions that it may contain, or for any misunderstandings arising from it.

www.ribapublishing.com

CONTENTS

Acknowledgements   iv
About the authors   v
Preface   vi

Part I: Making modular housing

1. Towards a modular architecture   3
2. A modern modular vernacular   29
3. Making a modular metropolis   51
4. Architects as designers in industry   77
5. Making sure it stacks up   99
6. The modular world   117
7. Building a more modular future   141

Part II: Modular case studies

Case study 1: Apex House   147
Case study 2: New Islington   157
Case study 3: Greenford Quay   165
Case study 4: Beechwood West   175
Case study 5: Mapleton Crescent   183
Case study 6: Union Wharf   193
Case study 7: Clement Canopy   199
Case study 8: George Street   205

References   220
Further reading   224
Index   225
Image credits   229

ACKNOWLEDGEMENTS

We would like to thank all the great people at HTA who have helped design and deliver some of the inspirational modular projects that have helped advance the industry and contribute to the success of our practice. It is because of their hard work that we were asked to write this book. Our thanks go to John Fleming and his team at Tide Construction and Vision Modular Systems for leading the way in defining the astonishing possibilities of modular housing. It is because of their hard work that there is even a need to write this book.

We are most grateful to Simon Toplis, Ronan Glynn, Kwame Ohene-Adu and Ana Raducu for sharing their expertise; to Mark Farmer and Donna Macfadyen from Cast Consulting for writing Chapter 5; and to architects Metropolitan Workshop, Assael Architecture and Pollard Thomas Edwards, as well as Michael Hough of MJH Structural Engineers, Maey Leow at TW-Asia and Aurélie Cleraux at Bouygues, for their contributions to the case studies.

Particular thanks go to Roanna Thetford and Nerea Bermejo for the inspiring illustrations; and to Rachel Hardman and Kate McFadden for their tireless work cataloguing the images and securing the appropriate permissions, through countless revisions.

Thanks also to Tom Bent at ETP Scotland for his assistance with research into embodied energy, to Henry Mickleburgh for information on international markets, and Dr Wei Pan at HKU for information on Hong Kong, and to Dickon Robinson and Claire Bennie for their own modular memories.

Thanks to Ginny Mills and Clare Holloway at RIBA Publishing for commissioning the book and for their patience and forbearance in managing us bringing it to a conclusion.

ABOUT THE AUTHORS

Simon Bayliss is an architect and urban designer with a passion for making better housing. He is managing partner of HTA, a practice that combines diverse talents across architecture, landscape, planning, interior design, engagement and research to create more sustainable homes and great places to live.

Rory Bergin is a partner at HTA, having trained as an architect in Dublin. He joined HTA to work in housing for 'a while' and stayed a couple of decades. He has worked primarily in sustainable design and prefabrication consultancy. He writes often in the architectural press and speaks regularly at conferences. This is his first book.

PREFACE

If we are to move towards the making of better housing in the UK, then we must first acknowledge the need for a revolution in the way we design, procure and deliver the housing we would all be happy to call home.

Housing is perhaps the most political of all building types. The quality, availability and affordability of housing is a fundamental factor in determining access to opportunity and a better quality of life, and it can have a significant impact on health and well-being. Yet the politics of housing is often reduced to a single number – the target of units to be delivered each year – without due consideration of the how or where. Meanwhile, an industry of mainly private sector companies, charged with delivering housing is forced to focus on a range of complex and competing standards that can reduce the most exciting and ambitious brief to multiple schedules of compliance.

Proposed new housing schemes are often met with the strongest resistance from existing communities, challenged by local people who should consider new housing to be a welcome benefit. The whole matter is then subject to our creaking planning system, through which local democracy is entrusted to adjudge on the balance of need, compliance and even beauty.

As it has also been said, usually by architects, that all architecture is political, then it is a wonder that the world of architecture and politics of housing have only intermittently managed to effectively interact and, more rarely still, to drive better outcomes.

Against this backdrop, a widespread acceptance that the UK is in housing crisis has at least driven politics and industry together again. This started with a need to seek solutions to reverse the long-term annual undersupply of new housing relative to historic levels and the consequent record high prices, making a decent home a dream for far too many. While the debate has at last moved on to the critical role of quality in achieving increased output, the challenge comes at a time when the industry could hardly be in a worse position to respond effectively and rapidly, as it faces its own crisis of quality failures, regulatory uncertainty, a chronic skills shortage and, particularly at the stage of construction, a culture based on behaviours that range between adversarial and aggression.

This books sets out the case for a technological revolution in housing, to build better through the design of modular housing that harnesses advanced manufacturing techniques. It seeks to demonstrate how technology and a culture that embraces innovation can begin to make a positive impact on housing delivery and the wider construction sector, as it has done in almost all other areas of modern life.

To move towards better outcomes we need to push for improved regulation and governance to find better ways for the entire team to combine their skills and motivations to create the homes individuals and families need, so that the nation can prosper, and deal with the real crisis of the global climate emergency.

If modernisation of the housing construction industry couldn't have come at a more important moment, it is also true that earlier periods of major innovation in housing themselves emerged in response to their own housing crises, often to suffer ignominious endings and then derail the process of modernisation for another generation. We are again, in the face

PREFACE

Fig 1
The tallest modular building in the world delivered by Tide Construction Ltd and Vision Modular Systems.

George Street, HTA Design LLP, London Borough of Croydon, 2020

of a new crisis, finding ourselves in urgent need to test whether we have found the right conditions for achieving a permanent state of progress.

Some of the enthusiasm for pursuing the goal of industrialisation has, very naturally, arisen from the expectation that only a modernised construction industry would have the potential to increase housing delivery to help us move closer to the ever-increasing housing target, currently set at some 300,000 new homes per year. But it has also gained traction for its potential to deliver better outcomes through increased focus on design and reduced defects on site, along with a considerable number of environmental benefits, and within a culture more conducive to enabling effective delivery, following the seemingly never-ending incidents of high-profile construction failures making the news.

The idea for writing the book came about as our practice, HTA Design, was completing the significant modular construction milestone with the redevelopment of Apex House in Wembley, north-west London. The project saw the completion of a 29-storey student housing scheme of 546 homes, from inception, through design, planning, manufacture, construction, assembly and handover to its new residents in an astonishing 30 months, with just under 12 months of that delivering the project on site. That we were working on our fourth consecutive project with the same developer and modular manufacturer, underlined the importance of a more collaborative culture, based on optimising the skills of the entire team and a partnership between designers and producers from beginning to end. So unlike many earlier texts on the subject this is not a book on the theory of what may be possible, but rather a demonstration of what has already been achieved over the past decade.

Since then, the need to write the story of the modular housing revolution has become ever more necessary with the convergence of factory-made housing and a new generation of purpose-built rented housing, and it has become easier with the significant increase in the number of completed projects around London. The past decade has seen the nation's relationship with housing shift from the single-minded pursuit of property ownership towards a more sophisticated understanding of the benefits of various forms of rented housing. In response, the private rented sector has sought to deliver better design and improved construction quality to provide housing customers would choose to live in, and within buildings in which owners and operators are happy to invest in.

Meanwhile, the rapid emergence of more suburban models of modular family houses is seeking to transform the landscape and offer better designed, better built homes, after decades of monopoly by volume housebuilders, not traditionally known to be receptive to driving innovation in the way they design or build.

The central theme for this book is the exploration of the wide-ranging benefits that a new approach can bring to the standard of design and quality of construction, to enable the production of higher performing buildings and to encourage a more collaborative industry. Only that way can we deliver better outcomes for everyone involved: the designers and producers, the funders, owners and managers, the local councils, the existing communities welcoming further investment in their neighbourhoods and, above all, to the benefit of the residents who will choose to live there.

This book explores the reason why there has never been a more propitious time for a revolution in modular housing, and sets out the case for an explosion in factory made housing. It is also a call to the architects and designers engaged in housing design to embrace better models for delivery and a much improved culture that could, perhaps quite counter-intuitively, provide the profession with the greatest opportunity of a generation to regain a more central role in the creation of better homes for our communities.

WE DEDICATE

this book to the modern pioneers of modular housing. Their commitment to great design and engineering excellence, their dedication to continuous improvement through research and development, and investment in factories to deliver homes that we can all be proud of, is showing the industry that it is possible to do much, much better.

PART I
MAKING MODULAR HOUSING

The first section of this book explores recent developments in modular construction and the dramatic progress in harnessing more advanced methods of manufacturing and assembly to drive better quality and more rapid delivery of housing across the UK and internationally.

Chapter 1 reflects on the history of invention and ambition in UK housing and the specific drivers over the past century and how a past culture of innovation had all but disappeared by the end of the 20th century across a housing industry unable, or at least unmotivated, to solve the country's chronic housing shortage.

Chapter 2 focuses on the volumetric modular systems for low-rise suburban family housing in the UK, building on the rich history of terraced housing to create a new generation of housing that has the character of favoured period homes, but designed to contemporary standards of performance and specification and offering greater customisation and choice to the customer.

From family housing to city centre living, **Chapter 3** explores the technical advancements of the past decade that has seen modular buildings increase in height from around 20 storeys to almost 50 storeys today. This sector has largely been driven by an increase in new forms of rented housing whereby institutional investors see the benefit of more rapid delivery and greater cost and programme certainty, as well as increasing evidence of a much reduced environmental impact compared to traditional construction. The pursuit of ever-increasing height has captured the attention of industry commentators with competition emerging between countries and developers hoping to demonstrate the benefits of their particular system – from Singapore, to Manhattan and London.

A central theme of the book is the potential impact on designers working within the world of modular housing and **Chapter 4** investigates the benefits and challenges for architects working as designers in industry. We explore how the process of designing buildings while working closely with manufacturers leads to changing behaviours in the design and delivery team that are more closely aligned with the car and tech industries.

Chapter 5 investigates the cost implications of making modular housing 'stack up' within a development industry that generally struggles with innovation, written by Cast, a built environment consultancy specialising in offsite construction. Their founding director Mark Farmer, the government's MMC champion, lifts the lid on why the wider benefits need to be considered to truly understand the cost impact of building better, building modular.

Chapter 6 looks briefly at the worldwide adoption of modular housing and highlights significant companies and projects which warrant further attention.

Throughout Part 1 we present a number of short case studies to demonstrate the past progress and future potential of modular made housing. We then look briefly ahead to future developments, before exploring several of the most significant recent projects through a series of detailed case studies in Part 2.

Facing page
The Journey - Modular construction by Nerea Bermejo Olaizola, HTA Design LLP

CHAPTER 1
TOWARDS A MODULAR ARCHITECTURE

As architects seek to create a new golden era for housing, the opportunity to drive more systemic change across the industry has scarcely been more possible, or more urgently needed. To succeed, the designers and manufacturers at the forefront of new construction solutions need to ensure they enable nothing short of a revolution in the way we produce our homes. Such systemic change would normally only occur through the setting of ambitious policy at national level, with government driving through new requirements through higher standards and regulations. In the absence of any bold new political vision, it is left to a small but influential group of clients, manufacturers and architects, to show the benefits of factory made housing, and modular housing in particular, through a growing number of completed developments. These projects are causing both industry commentators and policy makers to wake up to the opportunity. Although this quiet revolution has come from a small number of industry disruptors who see the opportunity to build in ways more appropriate to the technological advancements of the 21st century, in doing so they are finding major solutions to the far wider challenges facing the industry today. Above all, they are establishing an entirely new culture within construction, changing the nature of the relationship between client and producer, builder and designer, to the benefit of everyone involved.

'The entire Peabody board was motivated to find better ways of delivery. The aim was to seek ways to harness incremental improvements to avoid continually reinventing the wheel believing that every generation needs to try and see if their circumstances for delivering volumetric prefabrication have become more propitious'

Dickon Robinson, Director of Development, Peabody Trust 1988-2004

Facing page
Greenford Quay, HTA Design LLP, Ealing, 2019

WHAT CRISIS?

The current housing crisis has its origins in the early 1980s when, following a 25-year boom of housing construction very much driven by the public sector, the state promptly withdrew from its central role as a housing provider. This left new provision of housing almost entirely in the hands of a private sector focused primarily on the process of trading land, delivering houses that were little more than bricks and mortar with a primary focus of optimising returns for their shareholders. As politicians pushed the notion of property ownership as being central to individual prosperity and self-worth, the pace of delivery of new housing fell away and house prices climbed, all the while with design quality falling down the agenda as the housebuilders ensured architects and designers were entirely absent from their projects.

Although the beginning of this century saw new regulations for higher performance standards to ensure new homes would at least be warm, quiet, dry and safe, this coincided with increasing deregulation in the control of these standards, with compliance delegated to self-assessment by manufacturers and suppliers, and contractors increasingly focused on reducing cost and finding the most basic route to compliance.

As design and build became the dominant form of procurement, the role of the professional design team has become marginalised to the point that it rarely involves a meaningful engagement on site through the delivery of most projects. Meanwhile the role of the clerk of works, traditionally a key component in ensuring adequate oversight through the complex process of construction, is all but obsolete.

This has inevitably led to a race to the bottom across the sector as contractors compete on dangerously low profit margins while accepting wholesale transfer of risk for the project, are putting all qualitative aspects of the project continuously under threat. The outcomes of this have come to light through a series of high profile building failures, it's fair to say not just in the housing sector, but which reached a horrific apogee in the Grenfell Tower fire in 2016. This tragedy brought into sharp focus the crisis of poor quality in construction through fragmented responsibility in the process of oversight, and of an industry struggling to keep pace with the increasingly complex changes in regulation while constantly under pressure to reduce costs, without the capacity or culture to invest in more productive modes of operation.

Meanwhile, in a reversal of the trend of the past century, levels of home ownership have recently been in decline as prices have climbed and access to mortgage finance has hardened, leaving those not able to access a dwindling supply of social housing only able to rent from a poorly regulated private sector formed mostly of amateur and absent buy-to-let landlords.

It is now widely accepted across the political spectrum that housing delivery needs to increase to meet the nation's needs. In previous periods of housing crisis such complex and chronic problems provided a catalyst for positive government policy and enthusiastic private sector endeavour to align and provide the housing needed but often with negative consequences. Fortunately there are also signs that the government recognises that the focus on increased numbers also needs to address issues of affordability, quality, skills and sustainability. It is increasingly understood that failure to address these factors will not only prevent the delivery of more homes but also ensure that those built, will fail in delivering the housing the nation needs to enable future prosperity and good health.

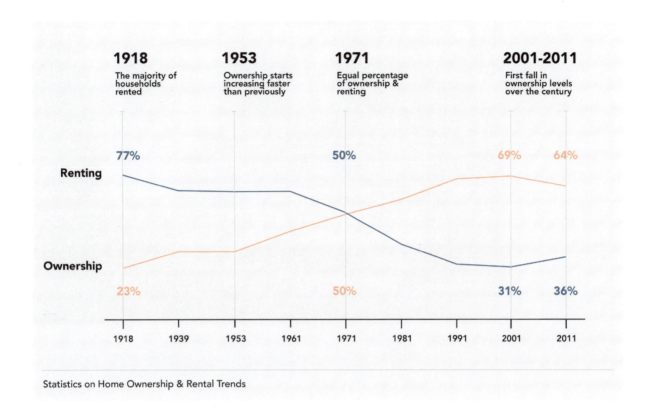

Fig 1
Statistics on home ownership and rental trends from the Office for National Statistics[1]

HOUSING BOOMS AND INNOVATION BURSTS

If a housing revolution is to be forged from industrialisation then it is surely important to learn the lessons of those that went before.

The UK has a rich history of housing design and delivery with some notable highlights that have impressed and influenced housing design around the world, along with some contrasting low points that despite their best intentions, have done much to set the industry back in its attempts to modernise and secure a brighter future.

Many consider the homes built in the first UK housing boom that finished a little over a century ago to still be amongst the best examples of mass housing across the world. The Georgian, Victorian and Edwardian periods all built huge numbers of homes across the whole of the UK, transforming most towns and cities in the process. These were mostly built speculatively by private developers, buying land and building homes often to widely adopted pattern books of house type designs that could respond to varying viability and changing markets, not to mention changing site conditions and local materials. Each period reflects the technological innovations of the time, with the compact Georgian terraces of the high density walkable city, built from manufactured bricks, of varying sizes and prefabricated joinery and with notable innovations such as the weighted sash window, still something of a marvel of beauty and functionality today.

The dawn of public transport enabled rapid urban expansion with houses a little more spread out to create wider and deeper homes, some terraced but also increasingly semi-detached and detached houses that promoted greater variety, but still through pattern books

to create the relatively compact suburbs for the rapidly expanding Victorian middle classes. Meanwhile the arrival of the railways moved labour, materials and manufactured products ever more easily and cheaply around the country, making York stone or Welsh slate universally available, while the standardisation of brick dimensions converged with standard housing layouts to create a form of mass production with endless customisation. Whole streets and neighbourhoods were made of just the right level of repetition and variation, with homes differentiated often by quite superficial modifications in detailing and finish. It is notable that architects were rarely involved in the design and delivery of such speculative housing, focusing instead on the individual homes for the wealthy patron, and yet many of these neighbourhoods formed of simple streets and squares have created such lastingly popular places, with elegant and flexible homes, that they have continued to steadily increase in appeal to this day.

Approximately 6 million homes were built during the Victorian period alone but notoriously not all met the high standards we still celebrate today. The huge demand for housing created by a rapidly urbanising population led to slum dwellings which through the chronic overcrowding of huge swathes of often unsafe and usually unsanitary houses, led to the first steps towards establishing housing as a human right, and as an essential element of a healthy and prosperous nation. A succession of housing acts from the mid-1860s seeking ways to encourage councils and wealthy philanthropists to improve the terrible housing conditionsof the poorest, led to a first era of state involvement in housing innovation.

HOMES FOR ALL

Fig 2
Typical London Georgian terrace

The 1919 Housing Act was perhaps the first major breakthrough in housing delivery as the state established itself as a major provider of the nation's housing. Driven by the widespread need to replace the poor conditions endured by many living in slum housing, and to provide

Fig 3
Interwar cottage estates

the homes for heroes returning from the horrors of World War I, the state built over 1 million council homes in the 20 years leading up to World War II.

But it was the arrival of the Labour Government in 1945 and the founding of the Welfare State which put housing alongside health and education as an essential element for creating a fairer society out of the destruction of global war. Housing need was driven by a dramatic growth in population coupled with the need to continue slum clearance and to replace the homes destroyed by war, which together provided a very straightforward narrative and widely accepted political imperative. Successive governments, both Conservatives and Labour, outbid each other to set the highest targets to impressive effect with a peak of just over 425,830 homes completed in 1968 under Harold Wilson's Labour Government, with over 40% being council housing.[2]

The period can be characterised as one of dramatic innovation in planning and construction which began with the introduction of new system-built family houses on the 'cottage estates' of the 1940s, adopting a range of panellised systems to help speed up construction using prefabricated components assembled and finished on site. This industrial process was in part due to a shortage of labour but it is notable that such innovation did also often help to reduce construction costs, in part because of the shortage of available labour.

Perhaps the most fondly recalled homes delivered during this early post-war period, and the most innovative, were the prefabs. Single-storey homes, intended to be temporary, but with many still standing and providing beloved homes decades later, they were perhaps *the* symbol of the government's commitment to rehouse the people quickly, but in homes of appropriate quality. Built by various manufactures to a range of systems they nonetheless all shared a similar design with each two bedroom bungalow constructed of four modules finished on site in a matter of days. They were the first fully modular homes in the UK, with rooms assembled and fully finished in the factory including all the 'mod cons'. Although only around 150,000 homes of this type were built under the Temporary Housing Programme between 1945 and 1949, it is a remarkable testament to the quality of design and robustness of manufacture that although built to last 10-15 years, some were still proving popular homes into the 21st century, over 50 years later.

But it was the 1960s when innovation in planning and construction really took off. Hailed as a golden era for housing, the decade saw New Towns being established, the adoption of the Parker Morris standards, and a succession of housing and planning acts all intended as political mechanisms to deliver new homes at scale and at will.

The fashion to build upwards was at first driven by pragmatic considerations such as the shortage of available land in city centres, alongside more visionary drivers around the optimism of a new generation of modernist planners and architects learning from continental Europe, and even suggestions from sociologists of the period that the inherent design of tower blocks could foster a sense of community.[3]

Fig 4
Prefab houses complete with fitted kitchen, delivered post war

TOWARDS A MODULAR ARCHITECTURE

Many early high-rise slab blocks and towers, particularly of the late 50s, were designed by notable architects with levels of inventiveness and attention to detail that resulted in good quality homes and buildings, that also formed successful and popular places. Many of these are still thriving over 60 years later.

The additional costs of building high were recognised by central government who provided generous subsidies to local councils tasked with procuring the housing. The Housing White Paper of 1963 set out the ambition to build 350,000 homes per year, and stated that 25% of them should be built using 'industrialised systems'.[4] In response, contractors hurried to offer innovative solutions that promised rapid delivery, and trouble-free procurement at a time when labour and materials were still in short supply, all within the parameters of the available subsidies. This was to lead to a rapid rise in prefabricated construction and a real boom in the building of both slab blocks and towers, the consequences of which were to last for decades.

While it is striking how similar the challenges of the day were to those that we face today, even if they are present for quite different reasons, the different attitude to the governments of then and now to facilitate change, is also equally of note.

Indeed government was to facilitate, through both enthusiastic endorsement and generous funding, the rapid procurement and construction by local authorities of housing schemes of increasing size and scale. The ability of private sector construction companies to respond with new solutions was undoubtedly impressive as they sought to harness innovation and technology that had emerged from the demands of war.

The boom of system-built high-rise construction was driven by a relatively small number of large contractors with companies such as Wates, Bison, Laing and Wimpey developing their own systems or purchasing rights to use systems from France and Denmark. As councils grew ever more ambitious to deliver numbers, the contractors saw the opportunity to harness industrialisation to short circuit the design process, offering package deals to councils based on off-the-peg solutions that removed the need for an architect or engineer, and further

Fig 5
Alton Estate, LCC Architects, London Borough of Wandsworth, 2001

reducing costs. The result was that by 1966 around 55% of public housing was delivered using package deals, and architects were increasingly excluded from the design of a built form they had previously enthusiastically supported and been instrumental in promoting.

As developments increased in size with ever more standardisation the potential for variety and design quality rapidly diminished, ultimately at great cost to future residents and councils faced with unsustainable maintenance requirements. There's no doubting the monumental scale of estates such as the Red Road flats in Glasgow, or the Aylesbury Estate in South London which redeveloped a 28-hectare site following slum clearance, to provide over 2700 homes within 16 blocks between four and 14 storeys. Constructed of prefabricated concrete panels from the Danish 12M Jespersen system based on simple multiples of a single standard dimension, the project was delivered by the construction company Laing, who had just recently completed construction of the M1 motorway.[5]

By 1968, enthusiasm had dimmed for the package deals due to the unappealing aesthetic and the rapid problems emerging from poor standards of construction. In May of that year, a gas explosion led to the partial collapse of Ronan Point, a tower block in East London, effectively sounding the death knell for the package deal and ultimately council housing delivered on a grand scale. Although some larger projects continued on to completion for some years, concrete and prefabrication were to become synonymous with all that was wrong with council housing and modernist ideals.

But it is important to acknowledge that collectively the various governments between 1945 and 1980 managed to complete a total of 5 million council homes, which would not have been possible without such innovation in design and construction. A huge majority of these homes were well designed and built to a high standard and remain attractive homes today. However, the period does stand as a reminder that building homes is a complex endeavour and that production techniques adopted from industries such as car production need to be applied with the utmost care and consideration.

Fig 6
Red Road Estate, Sam Bunton & Associates, Glasgow, 1960

Fig 7
Housing nearing completion

Aylesbury Estate, Department of Architecture & Planning, London Borough of Southwark, 1965

The arrival of the Thatcher Government in 1979 heralded the state's retreat from any significant role in housing delivery. Although mostly driven by an ideology that considered the market to be the primary mode of provision, it was not difficult to blame councils for the problems already established in some of the worst council housing of the previous years. Although delivery through a local authority-managed supply chain had its advantages in guaranteeing delivery, the negative impact of poorly designed prefabricated buildings using exposed concrete led to the housing industry taking a break from innovation for two decades.

THE ORIGINS OF THE MODERN MODULAR REVOLUTION

Towards the end of the 20th century it was acknowledged that all was not well in the UK construction industry, and commissions were established to investigate the problems and identify potential solutions. Sir Michael Latham's 1994 report 'Constructing the Team'[6] advised on better contract and procurement and then Sir John Egan's 'Rethinking Construction'[7] of 1998 advised on ways to improve the quality and efficiency of UK construction. The optimism of the new Labour Government in 1997 aimed to do better for housing and kick-started the competition for Greenwich Millennium Village, won by Countryside and L&Q to designs by HTA with Ralph Erskine. The proposal was to create more flexible and adaptable housing to meet the changing needs of a community over time, constructed using advanced modern methods of construction. In the end the industry simply lacked the capability to fully deliver on the proposals and ultimately more traditional modes of construction were adopted but for HTA the project was to set in motion a new period of investigation into the benefits of factory manufactured housing.

Fig 8
Greenwich Millennium Village, HTA Design LLP, London Borough of Greenwich, 2018

Murray Grove
Hackney, London

FACTS

Location	Murray Grove, Hackney, London, N1 7LT
Planning authority	London Borough of Hackney
Client	Peabody Trust
Contractor	Kajima
Modular manufacturer	Yorkon
Module construction	Steel frame
Architect	Cartwright Pickard
Start date	1997
Completion date	1999
Construction period	6 months
Number of homes	30 'key worker' homes
Number of modules	c. 90
Storeys	5

Completed just before the turn of the millennium during a period of optimism following the Egan Report 'Rethinking Construction' published a year earlier, Murray Grove provided some indication that construction in general, and housing delivery in particular, might be on the cusp of positive change. Built for the Peabody Trust, the scheme sought to overcome persistent problems with poor quality construction and programme overruns across their development programme. It provides 30 homes for 'key workers', a form of tenure introduced to provide housing for workers such as teachers, nurses or firefighters, who, though often on quite modest salaries, need to remain living in the city to ensure it continues to function effectively.

The project met expectations in almost eradicating defects and being completed to programme. Indeed the main problems affecting the build were reported to be problems with the traditionally built staircase not being fabricated correctly – several times. Nonetheless, the project was completed in just six months. For a truly innovative project, the first to deliver permanent housing to contemporary standards on a small urban site, the simplicity of plan and repetition of dwelling types enabled greater focus on overcoming logistical and management issues of something not done before. Perhaps entirely appropriately given the aspiration for Peabody to differentiate the project from the more typical and problematic traditionally built projects, the architectural approach chose to celebrate the construction methodology with an engineered aesthetic that celebrates the modular fabrication and means of assembly. The delineation of each module is quite clearly expressed within the facade system of terracotta planks that further celebrates the mode of construction.

The homes all proved incredibly popular as well as efficient and had low running costs due to the high standard of construction as well as sensible design decisions around orientation, aspect and access. The team considered every aspect of the design and to balance the repetition the entrance, balconies and components such as light fittings were all chosen carefully. Quicker, higher quality and understood to be of comparable costs to traditional construction the success of this scheme is clearly evident in the quality of the building after some 20 years of occupation.

Fig 9
Murray Grove, Cartwright Pickard, London Borough of Hackney, 1999

PUBLIC SECTOR INVESTMENT

One such successful response to recognised problems of quality in housing delivery was pioneered by one of the UK's oldest housing companies, the Peabody Trust. Seeking more certainty in cost and programme and higher quality with reduced defects, Peabody had the benefit of a significant development programme through which a series of projects would enable incremental improvements, combining standard elements with innovation that didn't require reinvention every time. A client initiative, driven from the Peabody board, but embraced in full by the architect, the two completed projects at Murray Grove by Cartwright Pickard and Raines Dairy by AHMM were ample demonstrations of an approach to buildings with a permanent and engineered aesthetic, which expressed their method of production but fully delivered on the expectations for improvement.

PRIVATE SECTOR INNOVATION

Meanwhile, seeking ways to invigorate the particularly inward-looking housing sector, Deputy Prime Minister John Prescott challenged the industry to embrace more modern methods of construction through the Design for Manufacture competition of 2005 which aimed to prove offsite construction as a route to quicker and cheaper construction. A series of public sector sites were made available but, reflecting the politics of the times, were subject to competitive bids by developers to purchase the opportunity to build and sell homes on the land, with the method of construction forming only a part of the criteria.

Although around 1000 homes were delivered on eight sites the post-completion evaluation acknowledged that the brief had perhaps been too complex, offering sites that were governed by varied design codes, along with the challenge of reducing costs, all while aiming to drive investment in costly manufacturing facilities. As a result, the level of manufacturing was variable at best, and there was little evidence of the competition driving any further innovation in the industry beyond the delivery of these sites.

The successor initiative was the Carbon Challenge, launched by John Prescott in 2008, which set clearer and somewhat more challenging criteria to meet the highest environmental standards including zero carbon. Although again configured as a programme of land disposals through which developers would build a mix of housing for sale and rental, the land value effectively paid the price for the innovation in construction and higher than typical standards. The programme was a casualty of the 2008 financial crisis but the first site at Hanham Hall, in a suburb of Bristol, was completed by 2013 and remains one of the largest zero carbon community in the UK. Designed by HTA, it was built using the high-performing Kingspan TEK system, factory produced to achieve the required levels of insulation and airtightness to help achieve sufficient thermal efficiency. Intended as a pilot project to help demonstrate that higher standards could be delivered in UK housing, the lessons were largely lost as standards were washed away by a change in government.

TOWARDS A MODULAR ARCHITECTURE

Fig 10
Design for Manufacture competition for Barratt Homes.

Allerton Bywater, HTA Design LLP, Leeds, 2012

Hanham Hall
Bristol

FACTS

Location	Hanham Hall, Bristol, BS15 3FR
Planning authority	South Gloucestershire Council
Client	Barratt Homes
Contractor	Barratt Homes
MMC manufacturer	Kingspan
Construction	Kingspan TEK
Architect	HTA Design LLP
Start date	2011
Completion date	2013
Construction period	2 years
Number of homes	185
Number of modules	n/a
Storeys	3

Hanham Hall is still a pointer to the way ahead for low-rise zero-carbon housing. Dense, green but immensely liveable, it showed how housebuilders could change their spots if they were willing to do so. The nine-hectare site adjoins the green belt, bordered by suburban housing with a grade II* listed hall which has been refurbished and successfully adapted to create a busy hub for the community with office space, a crèche and cafe.

The layout of the scheme responds to the site's unique characteristics and constraints with green belt restrictions and the need to retain views of the Hanham Hills meant more than a third of the site could not be developed. The house types were a function of the uniquely high performance standards and quality aspirations required by the brief.

The design stage involved advanced modelling and prototyping to ensure the project could meet the standards of energy reduction, through optimising daylight while avoiding overheating. The internal layout of the homes explored ideas around flexibility in use to meet the changing requirements of multigenerational living while allowing cross and stack ventilation with distinctive double height living spaces. The architecture expresses a connection of the homes to their natural setting with a large veranda combining with mono-pitch roofs which tilt upwards to maximise the southerly aspect of the homes and brings light into their living spaces.

TOWARDS A MODULAR ARCHITECTURE

Fig 11
Zero-carbon scheme for Barratt Homes.

Hanham Hall, HTA Design LLP, Bristol, 2014

Fig 12
Innovative housetypes with timber verandas.

Hanham Hall, HTA Design LLP, Bristol, 2014

The Kingspan TEK system was adopted to ensure high levels of insulation and airtightness using a precision manufactured envelope enabling all homes to achieve the new 'zero-carbon' standard. This enabled the homes to consistently improve on their design performance with the very first prototype achieving 0.9 air changes per hour, well beyond the target and what is typically possible with traditional on-site construction. Post-occupancy evaluation has shown that the housing performs above expected levels, and the method of construction has presented no issues or problems.

FIXING A BROKEN HOUSING MARKET

By 2016, government recognised that another review of the state of the construction industry was required, commissioning the 'Farmer Review of the UK Construction Labour Model'.[8] This was an investigation into the challenges facing the industry due to chronic lack of investment and worsening productivity and found the prognosis sufficiently bleak for the report to be subtitled: 'Modernise or die'.[9] Highlighting chronic failure to embrace modern technology, inconvenient patterns of on-site working and a poor safety record, the report blamed this lack of innovation and forward progress for the drop in workers entering construction. This pessimism was reinforced in a government report of the following year entitled 'Fixing our broken housing market', which acknowledged the widespread issues of a long-term undersupply of housing but, despite the intent suggested in the title, offered little in the way of solutions.[10]

In some respects the Grenfell tragedy in June 2017 has led to a galvanising of action, with the subsequent Hackitt 'Independent Review of Building Regulations and Fire Safety'[11] setting out the urgent need to update the regulatory framework for the design of buildings, along with improved quality control on site. This requires a reversal of the deregulation and culture of self-certification of the past decade, which has so evidently led to failures in the quality of design and construction. It also needs a new relationship between client and builder with a greater shared understanding of risk and appropriate allocation between parties.

But elsewhere government has woken up to the poor quality of design in much of the UK's housing, delivered by the dominant volume housebuilders, be it the individual homes or the places they create. Although some have shown themselves capable of delivering to incredibly high standards when mandated, the general level of quality in their 'standard product' house types are becoming the lowest common denominator in housing around the edges of our towns and villages. Despite the repetitive use of unimaginative and undersized homes, many are still built with an incredible number of construction defects.

It is difficult not to conclude that this poor quality has been enabled by a planning system damaged by the significant cuts over the past decade. The recent RTPI Raynsford Review of planning described the undermining of the planning system, one of the UK's most trusted institutions, a system urgently needing investment to ensure appropriate quality in the built environment and to rebuild the public's trust in the system.[12]

Finally, and most importantly of all, the increased acceptance of the global climate emergency and need for urgent change in our use of fossil fuel energy and carbon emissions, along with an improved understanding of the potential positive contribution that the construction industry could make, adds ever more impetus to the sense of urgency around quality and performance, as well as the need to increase housing delivery.

So here we are again, a housing crisis of huge complexity, but this time all of the making of an industry unwilling to see the benefits of building better, and of modern politics unable to make the brave decisions that the case for change so evidently needs.

A TYPOLOGICAL APPROACH

As previous generations understood, the production of good ordinary housing is in fact particularly well suited to harnessing mass production technologies. Most housing is made of the combination of required room types in relatively standard configurations. As the experienced housing architect knows only too well, they are also formed from the agglomeration of a mass of standard dimensions of relatively limited variation. Defined in the UK within documents such as the Nationally Described Space Standards (NDSS) or the more technical guidance contained within the Building Regulations, these set the limits of variation in the sizes of individual rooms and dwellings overall, as well as requirements for achieving appropriate standards for access, safety and servicing.

Further practical considerations such as the placing of furniture and the highly serviced areas of bathrooms and kitchens, and the incorporation of standard components such as windows and doors sized to meet requirements for access, ensure that most rooms are best suited to being regular in shape, as squares or rectangles, as well as regular in size.

The self-contained nature of each room provides the enclosing walls for structure and services, while the minimum areas, widths and heights ensure that most rooms, no wider than 4m overall to the outside of the structure, can easily be constructed as a 3D module and loaded on to the back of a standard lorry for delivery to site.

These standard dimensions of housing, manufactured in modular form, must then be configured and conjoined to make elegant buildings and beautiful places that provide the varied homes needed to meet our housing needs.

This standardisation is as relevant to the traditional terraced housing forms that benefit from the use of repeated house types to create coherent and elegant streets, as it is to the design of apartment blocks, be they mid-rise mansion blocks or high-rise towers. All benefit from the order that can be established through assembling repetitive elements, in both the plan and elevation, and in doing so meet the practical need in any building to stack structure and services.

The building of each individual room, as a repetitive modular component in a factory, can of course be built to a far higher standard in the controlled and safe environment of the factory floor, than could be possible in the variable and often chaotic conditions of the typical building site. Each room or collection of rooms are configured into individual highly finished modules, that can then be delivered to site for assembly. The more traditional elements of construction particular to each individual site can then be limited to foundations and services, cladding and finishing, highways and landscape.

HOUSING AS INVESTMENT

Over the past decade we have seen the emergence of new housing solutions that challenge traditional home ownership assumptions. As purpose-designed, built and managed rental accommodation delivered at scale has become established in the UK, bringing lessons from the USA and Europe, a new relationship is being established between the developer and their delivery team, and between operator and rental customer. With the success of purpose-built student housing already proven, particularly in urban centres, the model is now being applied at scale to general needs rental housing, and beginning to expand into intermediate forms of shared habitation such as co-living and older person living.

Of course, such rental models have plenty in common with the council housing model and those of the philanthropic housing companies discussed earlier in this chapter where the development is funded by stable rental returns and underpinned by the long-term value held in the building as an asset.

As a result of the current crisis of affordability becoming an increasingly political issue, the long-term borrowing constraints on the public sector have recently being softened allowing local authorities to enter the development market again. This is expected to facilitate

Fig 13
Build-to-rent development for Greystar.

Greenford Quay, HTA Design LLP, London Borough of Ealing, 2016

delivery of more affordable homes in response to widespread demand and increasing numbers of local councils are seeking to take control of housing provision again. Of course most have little experience in this area and are finding the construction industry's crisis over changing regulations and dwindling skills a serious barrier. Many are looking to new models of delivery again, though most will surely have a backwards eye on the problems arising from enthusiastic adoption of system building in the middle of the last century.

For private developers and councils who build to rent and retain a long-term interest in their built assets, balancing levels of capital investment in construction against long-term maintenance costs in use are very different to homes for private sale, where responsibility for maintaining the building is quickly passed on. Such considerations influence all forms of rented living as long-term maintenance considerations, quality and speed of construction all play a more important role in considering the approach to design and specification of the buildings, as much as the modes of procurement and construction.

It is a significant indicator of the growing acceptance of rented housing, that the industry has seen grand ambitions for housing delivery from companies not normally known for building housing. Construction companies such as Laing O'Rourke, with a proven track record of construction innovation, have been investing in the facility to deliver modular housing solutions. Meanwhile Legal & General, better known for managing pension funds and insurance, have also established their own housing manufacturing facility, that seeks to deliver higher quality housing and at scale, to benefit from the long-term investment of housing ownership.

Meanwhile, a quiet revolution is gaining attention and credibility as a select group of relatively small and unknown developers are leading through pockets of innovation across the sector. These innovators are demonstrating that there is a better way, one that requires an entirely new culture at the heart of the development process but one that can benefit everyone involved in and affected by the delivery of new homes across the country. While this innovation comes in many different forms of manufacturing-led construction, which we will explore in later chapters, the focus of this book is on the overwhelming benefits derived from fully volumetric, modular housing.

Chapter White City
London

FACTS

Location	10 Westway, Shepherd's Bush, London, W12 0DD
Planning authority	London Borough of Hammersmith and Fulham
Client	Chapter London
Contractor	Tide Construction Ltd
Modular manufacturer	Vision Modular Systems
Module construction	Steel frame and concrete slab hybrid
Architect	HTA Design LLP
Start date	February 2016
Completion date	August 2018
Construction period	18 months
Number of homes	306 student bedrooms
Number of modules	338
Storeys	7

Figs 14, 15, 16
Handset brick and cast stone make this building indistinguishable from other types of construction.

Chapter White City, HTA Design LLP, London Borough of Hammersmith and Fulham, 2018

Built on the site of the old Savoy Cinema near East Acton underground station this project demonstrates the versatility of modular schemes in unlocking sites that have been vacant for long periods of time and proven challenging to redevelop. Located within the Old Oak and Wormholt Conservation Area, an interwar garden suburb of mostly two-storey cottages, the site fronts on to the A40, at a busy junction with Old Oak Road.

The scheme is formed of two six-storey wings, stepping up a storey to a linking corner element that marks the main entrance and presents a rather unexpected feature to drivers descending the Westway en route into London. Taking its architectural cues from the art deco of the demolished Savoy Cinema and some features of the surrounding arts and crafts house, the facade combines stock bricks with cast stone and handset bricks with green glazed brick accents, all traditionally laid on site, to create a horizontal and vertical layering that creates hierarchy across the long facades made of quite repetitive elements.

These facade materials, combined with the zinc clad dormer windows within the pitched roof on both wings, belie the technologically advanced modular building within. The living accommodation was fully finished in the factory with individual rooms fitted with furniture and only common areas including a cafe, student lounge, arcade and gym were finished on site.

To the rear of the building a sunken courtyard adds two additional storeys to incorporate building plant and services and communal amenities. This created a challenging interface between the concrete structure, transfer slab and the modules.

THE MODULAR HOUSING HANDBOOK

Fig 17
Vision Modular Systems' technologically advanced factory in Bedford

FASTER, SAFER, SMARTER, BETTER

Although it is possible to conceive of a time in the not too distant future when housing factories will feature highly automated production lines equipped with robots and advanced 3D printing technology, more typical modern modular housing manufacture simply relocates traditional construction to the safe and controlled environment of the factory floor. Production uses many traditional materials – steel, concrete, timber and plasterboard, combined with tested components – bathroom and kitchen fittings, plumbing and wiring, doors and windows, all assembled by a mix of traditional tradespeople, specialist factory operatives and unskilled workers trained and overseen in the controlled factory environment.

Working within the controlled and safe environment of the factory floor provides greater appeal to attract new workers, over the temporary and tough nature of working on site. Factory workers have more certainty of employment and work local to their home, making it easier to balance with busy modern lives. As a result the workforce is more diverse and the average age typically much lower, while equally facilitating later retirement.

The benefits for the project are just as significant, with potential for much reduced programmes helping to bring forward occupation and reduce disruption for the existing local community. Site work is also reduced with far fewer vehicle movements and leads to a quieter cleaner site while waste levels are dramatically reduced as the factory manufactures only what it requires, within an environment where it is far easier to recycle any waste made.

The combination of these factors – less material, fewer vehicle movements, reduced waste – also enables modular buildings to require far less energy to construct and involves

TOWARDS A MODULAR ARCHITECTURE

Fig 18
Wembley Modular schemes delivered by HTA Design LLP, Tide Construction Ltd & Vision Modular Systems

much reduced levels of embodied carbon. This is a compelling case in response to the climate emergency where manufactured buildings are already capable of meeting the standards set within RIBA's 2030 Climate Challenge.

DESIGN FOR MODULAR MANUFACTURE

For some architects, the idea of working within the constraints of any system might be considered an intolerable imposition and a threat to their creativity. However, the opportunity for modular construction for architects needs to be seen through the prism of the diminishing status of the profession over the past three decades, and in particular the marginalisation of the housing architect in the delivery stages of housing projects. The architect remains one of the few design professionals of the modern age not fully integrated with the production team, but it can not be argued that keeping apart from production has brought any benefit to the status or influence of the architect's role.

It is possible to conclude that in some respects, the quality of housing design has much improved in the UK over the past 20 years. Housing has again come to be considered one of the more important and rewarding areas of architectural practice, with the quality of architectural design quite evident in the archives of the annual Housing Design Awards.[13] Furthermore, David Birkbeck, Chief Executive of Design For Homes, organisers of the awards, has long organised study trips from the UK to view the best housing in Europe but of late has seen more visits from Europe to view innovation and design in the UK. However, it is notable

Fig 19
Interior visualisation of the 44th floor fitness room and roof terrace

that the increase in design quality has been confined to either higher value areas where planners are adequately funded and land values mean developers can afford to pay for more, or where a landowner, often from the public sector, sets a higher standard of compliance.

To change housing for the better right across the country, we have to engage in models that enable better production and across more varied tenures, and forge a different relationship with those who share the endeavour of the typical designer, to innovate, improve and advance.

For architects working with manufacturers, the design process becomes one of continuous collaboration from beginning to end and with greater potential to invest across a number of projects. Manufacturers are inherently driven by innovation and always seeking to improve quality through better design but are also focused on delivering outputs - in this case completing buildings - rather than seeking a planning consent to increase the value of land. Architects need to design efficient and elegant solutions that naturally optimise the potential of the site, but also develop resolved and costed schemes that will enable a rapid and seamless move into production and delivery. The design cycle is more iterative, with technical compliance and the logistics of delivery playing a greater role in the design, as they do in other design focused industries. This is explored further in Chapter 4 where we explore the idea of architects as designers in industry.

As the development cycle is driven by the need to maintain factory throughput, projects progress rapidly, cities are improved dramatically and local authorities welcome you back for the next project.

Through more effective engagement and alignment with the rest of the industry, architects can play a central role in transforming the way better homes are delivered. The profession has the opportunity to establish a more positive relationship with those that commission and construct housing, and put the importance of design centre stage, and enhance the role of architects as leaders in creative innovation.

To do so would bring untold benefits to society and influence wider solutions to a global problem and, just maybe, usher in a new golden age of housing.

Fig 20
Street level view of George Street, delivered by Tide Construction Ltd & Vision Modular Systems.

George Street, HTA Design LLP, London Borough of Croydon, 2019

CHAPTER 2
A MODERN MODULAR VERNACULAR

For the UK in particular the predominant form of new housing remains relatively low-density family houses and low-rise apartments in suburban and semi-rural locations. Usually linked to existing settlements as extensions to towns and villages it is a market dominated by a small number of high-volume housebuilders whose model for driving down cost involves plenty of repetition but only occasionally any innovation. As housing delivery has increased over recent years concerns have grown over the poor quality of homes being used to carpet over the land.

In 2018 the Ministry of Housing, Communities and Local Government held their Design Quality Conference,[2] which challenged the industry to do better, following which it launched the Building Better, Building Beautiful Commission, with the remit to 'advise government on how to promote and increase the use of high-quality design for new build homes and neighbourhoods'.[3] This is a market clearly in need of serious disruption.

Luckily, a generation of new developers are emerging with strong ideas about good design to challenge the status quo, while architects continue to investigate new approaches to housing design that can respond to climate change and modern modes of living. It is no accident that they are also focused on challenging modes of delivery and driving more innovative forms of construction.

Here we trace recent developments in manufacturing low-rise housing, harnessing various approaches to factory manufacture including use of steel and timber frames, structural insulated panels (SIPs) and fully volumetric modularised construction, as well as looking into changes to procurement and housing tenures such as Custom Build and Build to Rent, that are helping to drive forward improvements.

'[Housebuilders] must significantly raise their game if we are to create the sorts of places that future generations will feel proud to call home. It's no wonder so many of our communities feel apprehensive towards new development when the design is so poor. That's why significantly improving the quality of design is central to addressing the housing shortage.'[1]

UCL for CPRE and the Place Alliance, 2020

Facing page
New Islington, shedkm,
Manchester, 2019

THE MODULAR HOUSING HANDBOOK

Fig 1
Home of the Future, HTA Design LLP, 2015

Figs 2, 3
Floor plans showing the effect of no skylights (left) and with skylights (right).

Home of the Future, HTA Design LLP, 2015

Fig 4
The Hundred House,
HTA Design LLP, 2018

A VERY STANDARD PRODUCT

Low-rise housing in the UK has long been regarded as the Cinderella of innovation and progress in construction. Dominated by volume housebuilders who make money by buying land at relatively low prices and then building homes on it to sell to private buyers at high prices, it is an inherently conservative industry. The way large housebuilders build plays little part in determining their profits, and improvements in speed or quality are not fundamental to their business.[4] Consequently, they resist change and have successfully lobbied government on many occasions to delay or cancel legislation aimed at improving the environmental performance of homes.[5]

Despite the wide range of manufactured systems available to the UK housing industry, few of them are used at scale by the major housebuilders, with use of prefabrication generally limited to panel systems, which has a relatively minor impact on housing delivery.

More recently some are investigating increased prefabrication measures either due to increasing labour and skill shortages, or as public sector organisations such as Homes England, the UK Government's housing agency, mandates increased use of Modern Methods of Construction (MMC) on their sites being sold to private sector developers.

Although it seems unlikely that the industry will be motivated to change from within, there are recent signs that it may be changed by external disruption, in part caused by the threat of Brexit and the expected reductions in the traditional workforce due to retirement. The recent arrival of Japanese housebuilder Sekisui House in the UK with an investment in Urban Splash Modular provides some indication that dramatic change may be imminent.[6]

Many people rightly question whether factory production can really be relied upon to provide the answers it has failed to do before, posing the quite legitimate question – 'What is different this time around?' Given the legacy of 1960s system buildings and more recent failures such as the CASPAR building in Leeds,[7] what is to stop the same thing happening again?

For a conservative industry many are cautious of previous unsuccessful attempts to solve the manufacturing problems. Perhaps most notably Barratt Homes, the UK's largest housebuilder, set up the Advance factory in partnership with Terrapin in 2002 to build low-rise housing, in particular focused on the affordable housing sector. Adopting a 'pod and panel' approach the system was based on a high level of repetition for a limited number of house types and ultimately was not able to cope with the complex demands placed on housing development by the planning system and the factory closed in 2007.

The answer is to be found in much increased levels of investment, a real imperative to succeed due to increasing problems with traditional buildings, and as a result sufficient and growing competence in the industry to guard against such problems.

Furthermore, following a number of high-profile building failures over recent years, largely on traditionally constructed buildings, it seems likely that the industry will be required to increase oversight of standards and testing. This should result in a greater emphasis on design and construction quality, an advantage that manufacturers would do well to exploit by promoting the benefits of factory made housing.

However, factory production has made huge progress in its use of technology and process engineering, resulting in greater accuracy and better quality control. There is also substantially increased expertise within the engineering profession and design tools such as Building Information Modelling (BIM) that help to better coordinate design and prevent manufacturing failures. The industry is young however, and the stakes are high. New entrants to the market will need scrutiny and clients should require full accreditation with new innovations to be robustly tested before implementation.

INDIVIDUAL CHOICE, MASS MARKET APPEAL

For one-off entrants into the housing market such as the self-builder, who may only build one home in their lives, using some level of prefabrication represents a less risky approach as the supplier provides the system and installs it on site to a fixed cost and programme. In many countries a supply chain exists to meet such expectations.

The popularity of TV shows like 'Grand Designs' demonstrates the interest in society in a newly built and well-designed home, but choices in the UK are limited. German manufacturer Huf Haus has become well known for its high performance and bespoke specification timber-framed homes. Configured from a range of standard typologies the homes are precision manufactured and efficiently assembled to each individual customer's requirements. A high proportion of Scandinavian housing is also factory produced albeit largely using timber frame or panels, but these are all focused on one-off homes, within low density developments.

For local authorities in the UK who are returning to housing development, thanks to changes to rules for borrowing, prefabrication offers similar benefits and for curiously similar reasons. Many local authorities have lost the development knowledge that they once had and are unlikely to get it back quickly as such skills are in short supply. As a result they need a simple procurement approach that can speed up delivery and provide certainty of cost, while improving quality. After all, they will own and maintain the property for many years to come. Many local authorities have formed joint venture companies or wholly owned housing companies to deliver new homes on their own land, and some are looking to use offsite systems to deliver.

PLACE/Ladywell
Lewisham, London

FACTS

Location	Ladywell, London, SE13 6AY
Planning authority	London Borough of Lewisham
Client	Lewisham Council
Contractor	SIG Build Systems
Modular manufacturer	SIG Build Systems
Module construction	Cross-laminated timber
Architect	Rogers Stirk Harbour + Partners
Start date	August 2014
Completion date	September 2016
Construction period	6 months
Number of homes	24
Number of modules	48 (two per unit)
Storeys	4

Fig 5
Nearing completion.

PLACE/Ladywell, Rogers Stirk Harbour + Partners, Lewisham, 2016

PLACE/Ladywell is a scheme of 24 temporary homes designed by Rogers Stirk Harbour + Partners and built by SIG for Lewisham Council on a vacant site in Ladywell. With an increasing number of families in poor quality temporary housing, this provides a route to better quality accommodation as an interim to accessing more permanent housing.

There were three key objectives. Firstly, to provide 24 homes for homeless families living in poor quality temporary accommodation. Secondly, to create community commercial space at the ground floor. Thirdly, to infill a prominent site on the high street which had been left empty following the demolition of the Ladywell Leisure Centre and to act as a catalyst for future regeneration.

The design proposed the construction of a re-deployable building up to four storeys in height to provide 24 two-bedroom flats with up to four community/retail units at street level. After four years on the Ladywell site, the scheme will be relocated elsewhere within the borough. In the long term the buildings may find a permanent site, or may be divided up to create smaller projects according to site availability.

PLACE/Ladywell takes advantage of volumetric, factory manufactured construction techniques to build high-quality housing for Lewisham Council to a short programme and for reduced costs. The units are manufactured from standard timber components using simple technologies and then fully fitted out with bathroom, kitchen, flooring and all finishes in the factory. This gives the manufacturer full control over quality, finish and programme as well as reducing construction time, waste and noise on site.

This offsite manufacturing approach provides further advantages. The programme is significantly reduced resulting in lower construction costs, a key factor in the viability of the project for the council. Waste is minimised, and in addition to the use of timber as the primary construction material, the building is far more sustainable than a traditional building. It allows for greater client flexibility, creating spacious and affordable homes for its residents while addressing important social issues.

Fig 6
The drawing of the 4 storey deployable building on a vacant site.

PLACE/Ladywell, Rogers Stirk Harbour + Partners, Lewisham, 2016

UNDERSTANDING THE SYSTEM

There is a wide range of prefabrication systems available for the suburban housing developer with the most widely used being frame and panel systems which, while improving efficiency, do not significantly improve the speed or quality of any project. A structural frame can be as little as 10% of the project value, so can only modestly impact on either speed or quality but clearly the more complete the panel system, the greater the potential benefits. Combining panels together to make 3D volumetric modules that enclose whole rooms enables services, fittings and finishes to be installed in the factory, improving the quality of the construction elements that are most complex to coordinate and the most troublesome to deliver on site. These more advanced systems have increased benefits over simple panel and frame buildings, which have after all been around in various forms for centuries, but the complexities of manufacturing and delivery also increase considerably.

TIMBER FRAME

Timber frame is the default construction system in Scotland and is increasing its penetration into the market in the rest of the UK with the proportion of timber frame housing steadily increasing in England, reaching 27.6% by 2015 and still growing.[8] But this represents the simplest and most basic of the offsite technologies available. Despite some setbacks to the industry during its history it is now a mature technology with a substantial number of factories well distributed across the UK and Ireland supplying the housebuilding sector. It can be further broken down into as three similar technology types:

Open panel

Much of the supply is relatively low-tech, with open timber frames supplied as floor height elements to be erected on site. Prefabricated web joists and trusses are used to make the construction of low-rise houses quicker. The frame must be completed quickly and clad in weatherproof linings to protect it from weather and the danger of fire.

Closed panel

A small proportion of the market supplies timber frame panels with insulation and lining already applied to the panels. While this does speed up construction, it has been slow to gain traction while there has been cheap labour to apply the insulation and linings on site. There are substantial benefits to be gained in terms of airtightness and better building performance from using closed panels, as they tend to be of higher quality, due to better factory processes than can be achieved on site.

Structural insulated panels (SIPs)

SIPs are typically constructed from layers of insulation bonded to a lining board. The Kingspan TEK system uses a foamed insulant and two layers of oriented strand board (OSB) to achieve a structural panel. Because the insulation and panel are bonded, the two behave as a single structural element. SIPs are similar to closed panel timber frame but provide higher performance and quality benefits and can result in the construction of a small weather-tight home within a matter of days.

LIGHT GAUGE STEEL (LGS)

Like timber frame, LGS panels are supplied as open panels to site and then connected together to create a structural frame. The major advantage of this over timber frame is its lack of movement post construction and a reduced fire risk during construction. Some system manufacturers supply frames with the insulation installed, similar to a closed panel or precast concrete panels.

PRECAST CONCRETE PANELS

There are a number of manufacturing systems involving precast concrete panels where large-scale elements are used to form walls, floors, columns and balconies. These have similar benefits to CLT in terms of speed but carry an environmental penalty in terms of the CO_2 produced during construction. They bring other benefits, however, in terms of fire performance, robustness and acoustic performance.

CROSS-LAMINATED TIMBER (CLT)

This is a form of engineered timber made in factories, usually in Austria, Germany or northern Italy, where many weak timber elements are glued together in rows in opposing directions to form large thick panels that are structurally rigid. Panels can be up to 6x3m or even larger, which means that the system lends itself well to buildings formed of large cellular spaces where speed is beneficial. Many new schools have been constructed using this method in the UK and as the amount of construction increases, the costs will reduce.

MODULAR VOLUMETRIC SYSTEMS

Modular construction is the most advanced form of offsite construction with the highest level possible of pre-manufactured value and our main focus in this book.

There is a nostalgic memory in the UK of prefabrication in low-rise housing from the post-war prefabs built to quickly rehouse people from bomb damage and slum clearance as well as provide work to factories no longer needed for wartime production. The experience of steel manufacturing naturally led to many factories focusing on steel systems as the materials and skills were readily available.

Today the majority of companies active in the UK market still use light-gauge steel panels to manufacture three-dimensional frames which are then clad internally and finished using relatively traditional materials and processes. Many companies have found that using a hot-rolled cage to add extra strength to the frames has made them easier to transport and also to build taller buildings without having to change the basic structure of their modules. Some manufacturers incorporate a thin concrete slab floor within the modules to assist with fire and sound separation.

There are also companies specialising in timber-based modular construction. Some use variations on timber framing and others use CLT, solid timber panels that combine structural and insulating properties as well as reducing the levels of energy required for production and the carbon embodied in the building.

A MODERN MODULAR VERNACULAR

THE METRICS OF THE MODULAR HOUSE

It is typical of suburban family housing to be based around greater repetition of types and scales as the character of neighbourhoods is created through compositions formed of collections of houses, rather than the individual buildings.

The typical suburban family house, the home of choice for much of the UK population, is usually built on its own plot, with its own front door and with living rooms at the ground floor. It is usually two or three storeys tall and in the main, having two, three or four bedrooms: these would be located on the upper floors. Whether arranged as detached, semi-detached or higher density terraces, experience from over two centuries of refining these typologies has helped establish some key dimensions that enable each home to be designed efficiently and in compliance with relevant standards. Terraced conditions in particular are most defined by the width with principal living rooms needing to be a certain width to function, ideally no less than 3.5m, along with entrances, stairs and certain specific requirements for accessible ground floor WCs. Combined, a reasonable minimum width would probably be 4.6m internally, which when including an external wall on each side, requires an overall width of 4.8m to 5.0m. This is within the upper limits placed on the transportation of the modules without the need for additional permits or escorts and so a practical constraint which most manufacturers choose to work within. The standard ceiling height of good quality housing is typically set at a minimum of 2.5m, which with a 300mm floor zone forms a 2.8m floor to floor, well within the limits of transportation while the length forms no constraint, as a typical terraced home might expect to be no deeper than around 10m, well within the 18m maximum transportation limit.

In basic compliance terms, a two-storey, three bedroom, five person house, meeting the Nationally Described Space Standards, would need to be a minimum of 93sqm, or 46.5sqm on each floor. Based on a 4.8m wide internal width, and a corresponding length of 9.7m and an external dimension of around 5x10m.

Fig 7
Modularising the traditional terrace house

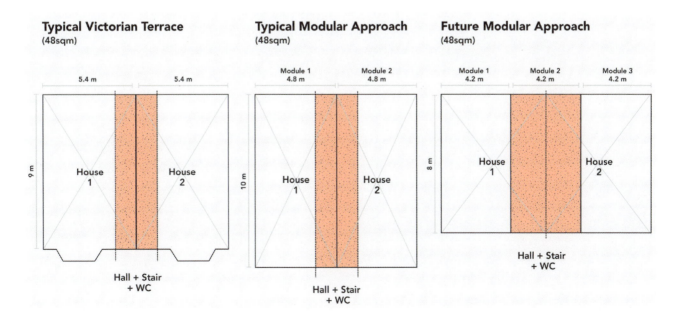

Building on these basic criteria, there is then no end of creative variety that designers can bring to bear on the problem, working with the manufacturers to understand and optimise other characteristics of the system and to work within manufacturing logistics.

MAINSTREAMING MODULAR

Other UK companies such as Portakabin, Wernick and McAvoy have been providing ready-made three-dimensional rooms or volumetric modules for use as temporary accommodation for some decades. Portakabin in particular became synonymous with the manufacture of 'temporary' additional classrooms to meet sudden changes in school size, some of which remained in use for decades. More recently these companies have seen the opportunity to apply their expertise to manufacture similar steel-framed or timber-framed systems to create fully finished rooms in factories for more traditional permanent low-rise housing.

Added to this group a notable number of new housing manufacturers have become active in the market and we present here a list of some of the most high profile companies, many of whom have received recent investment to enable them to grow and meet the demands of a rapidly changing market.

HOUSE/URBAN SPLASH MODULAR

A serial disrupter in the development of housing in the UK, often going where other companies fear to tread, it is no surprise that when Urban Splash made the decision to move into more family focused houses, they chose to adopt a modular solution. Built to designs by architect shedkm, the homes are based on a standard footprint with a range of options for internal configuration of the main spaces to suit the purchaser's needs and way of life. Further choice is offered through level of specification for fixtures, fittings and finishes. The first scheme in New Islington was delivered in partnership with SIG, following which Urban Splash acquired the factory and rebranded as Urban Splash Modular.

More recently the company has been successful in winning several contracts to deliver schemes on Homes England sites as well as continuing to grow its own development pipeline. The news that Sekisui House, the Japanese housebuilder and leading manufacturer of both mass-produced and one-off bespoke homes using factory production, has invested in them demonstrates their strength of position in the UK housing market.[9]

Fab House
North Shields

FACTS

Location	Smith's Dock, North Shields, NE29 6DG
Planning authority	North Tyneside Council
Client	Urban Splash and Places for People
Contractor	USC (Urban Splash Construction)
Modular manufacturer	Urban Splash Modular (as SIG)
Module construction	Timber frame
Architect	TDO Architecture and George Clarke
Start date	October 2017
Completion date	March 2018
Construction period	7 months
Number of homes	10
Number of modules	20
Site area	910sqm

Fab House is a new modular house typology designed by TDO and George Clarke for joint venture developers Places for People and Urban Splash. Constructed by SIG Homes, the factory now owned by Urban Splash, the terrace of 10 houses is part of a larger development. Each house is formed from a pair of stacked modules placed onto a pre-prepared traditional foundation. The distinctive grey fibre-cement panels and window and door surrounds set the design apart from its surroundings and give it a strong modern architectural character.

Fig 8
Fab House, TDO Architecture
& George Clarke, Manchester,
2018

ILKE HOMES

A company born from a joint venture between Elliott, a manufacturer of prefabricated buildings, and Keepmoat, a housebuilder and contractor, is a volumetric housing manufacturer based in Knaresborough with a fully functioning factory capable of producing 2000 homes per year. ilke has invested heavily in R&D and the recent news that it has signed a supply deal with Places for People to manufacture 750 homes for them is an indicator of how the industry has the potential to scale up, with large developing landlords and housing associations buying direct from factories instead of using traditional contractors.[10]

SWAN NU BUILD

Set up by Swan Housing Association to improve the quality of the homes they deliver across Essex and East London, Swan NU Build established the NU Living Factory, a CLT based modular production line, in Basildon in 2017 with the first homes produced the following year. The factory now builds low-rise and mid-rise housing for the Swan development programme which includes homes of all tenures and is expected to develop the capacity to add steel-frame modular to their production line for taller buildings. NU Build's approach is particularly interesting for the ability it offers customers to adapt their home online before it goes into production. Choices include the basic configuration of living space and bedrooms, kitchen type, storage, window colours and external brick type, as well as external additions and extensions.

LEGAL & GENERAL HOMES

The decision by leading pension and insurance firm Legal & General to enter the housing industry as a developer reflects the growing market for quality rental housing, backed by institutional investors seeking secure returns over the long term. Perhaps more surprising was their investment in a large modular housing manufacturing facility outside Leeds with the potential to deliver 3500 homes per year. These would be predominantly traditional two-storey family homes in suburban developments, with some low-rise apartments, and would be owned and managed by the company to provide long-term rental income. This whole-life model with a single company acting as developer, builder, owner and manager provides the opportunity to significantly change the way we view housing in the UK and, in theory at least, drives a new quality agenda based on longer-term investment. Production has been delayed from the initial launch date but it is anticipated that completions may start in 2020.

TOPHAT

A new entrant into the UK construction sector, TopHat is also a volumetric manufacturer of timber-framed low-rise housing based in Derby. The recent news that they have had a £75m investment from Goldman Sachs is an indicator of the interest from venture capitalists in the future of housing.[11]

AN EXPANDING MARKET OF INNOVATORS

Alongside these more established companies there is a large group of smaller innovators seeking to establish themselves in the market such as Actavo, F1 Modular, Ideal Modular, ESS Modular, Innerspace, NHouse, Premier, Totally Modular and Hatch Modular, all with the ambition of improving housing delivery through modular factory production.

THE MODULAR HOUSING HANDBOOK

SECURING A SUFFICIENT SUPPLY

For manufacturers to succeed they need to establish efficient factory production, with a sufficient pipeline of orders to function economically. A factory carries a large overhead of permanent staff and therefore needs a regular throughput to maintain a cost-effective production line and stay in business. While the benefits of factories are extensive, managing a fluctuating workload against the often unpredictable process of development is certainly one of the barriers to success.

Efficient production requires considerable coordination between the factory, the construction site and commissioning clients to ensure that the factory is neither idle nor overwhelmed. This requires commitment from clients and designers to enable delivery, and an understanding of the implications of delays arising due to planning approvals, design information release, securing a vacant site or development funding. The traditional approach of tendering construction projects to secure the lowest price not only fails to take account of the benefits of factory made homes, but also works against securing the benefits of such an approach.

Traditional tendering defers selection of a builder until very late in the development process, following which, building is expected to happen immediately and at breakneck speed. Engagement with a suitable manufacturer instead at the early stages can enable a design for manufacture and assembly (DfMA) approach to the whole project, which in turn will enable the project to achieve best value by designing in accordance with principles that suit the requirements of production, potentially also at the lowest cost by enabling standardisation.

STANDARDISED CUSTOMISATION

Fig 9
ilke Homes house type.

Hawthorne Avenue, MPSL, Hull, 2018

Fig 10
ilke Homes internal view of the Dalby house type.

Chase Farm, Keepmoat Homes, Nottinghamshire, 2018

Fig 11
Beechwood West, Pollard Thomas Edwards, Basildon, 2019

Fig 12
The Hundred House, HTA Design LLP, 2018

The issue of standardisation can of course be a challenging one for many architects who fear the potential loss of influence over design decisions and the stifling of their creative endeavours. This is perhaps a natural reaction given the marginalisation of architects from much of the UK's housing and the poor quality of many standard house types and unimaginative layouts delivered by many major housebuilders.

However, the reality is that standardisation is more often the answer to improved design quality as individual well-designed elements and components can be continuously refined and the process of both manufacture and assembly improved. This is as true for the performance of a particular wall build-up, as it is for the functionality of a utility cupboard, the most appealing proportions of a living room or the quality of light in a kitchen. This is inherently understood by most design professionals working in automotive or product design, and offers a huge opportunity for the architect and in any case, standardisation of process does not require everything to be the same.

Most successful housing manufacturers recognise that their systems must be capable of delivering buildings that fit on odd-shaped sites and that the residential market requires variety. Successful residential places develop often from a limited palette of similar sized homes, a set of materials that are used with minimal variation, along with a variety of vernacular details that are used with variation over a period of time. Many housing typologies that are widely used by housebuilders, developers, kit home suppliers or custom builders are based on some elements of standardisation. It may be invisible, but it's there. The holy grail of standardisation is the ability to then customise aspects of the outcome to best suit the customers' needs. People are satisfied with other products that are based on a family of types or sizes – such as cars or computers – that share common platforms based on a common specification. Such systems have developed to allow for a large range of customisation by the eventual purchaser. This is usually achieved by a sales process that guides the purchaser through a questionnaire or interview about their needs and then a set of choices are offered that meet those needs; the customer navigates these choices either online using digital configuration tools or with a sales agent to help to make decisions.

Long acknowledged to be well ahead of the game in manufacturing customisation, Japan meets much of its housing demand through a small number of factories which offer prefabricated housing based on a common platform with a wide range of customisation available. Although they dominate the market like the volume housebuilders do in the UK, the difference is they offer a custom-made home for each customer. Highly automated, individual manufacturers have the capability of producing up to 60,000 homes annually, approximately one-third of the total annual UK housing production.[12] This is compared to the UK where the largest offsite housing company can produce fewer than 4000 homes each year. Japan is a mature market where customers expect high quality and rapid production while also demanding a home that is bespoke to their needs. They are getting a fully designed one-off home, but they don't have complete freedom in the choices they are being offered.

CUSTOM BUILD VARIATION

On the Heartlands project at Trevenson Park, Pool, Cornwall, and other sites across the UK, Igloo formed a panel of designers/manufacturers to work with them on Custom Build projects. Customers buy a plot of land from Igloo, and then buy a customised home from one member of the panel that will be constructed on the land. The standardisation is in the size of the plot and the arrangement of the homes to fit on plots adjacent to each other and to form sensible urban and suburban streets. A design code is required to create some simple rules within which each manufacturer operates to enable this to work easily.

This process builds on the work done in other countries, most notably in Almere in the Netherlands where a much larger project is underway to allow thousands of homeowners to buy plots and construct the home of their dreams.

Modern manufacturing can cope more easily with ranges of sizes than older factories could, but it is less easy to cope with a range of connections or interfaces in a factory. While there is no difficulty in offering choices in the length and height of elements, there is a lot of complexity in offering choices in how those elements connect to each other. The technical requirements of building – in the same way as there are technical requirements in making cars or computers – mean that those parts are not available for flexibility, but the lengths between interfaces, heights of rooms, layout of rooms and internal and external finishes as well as kitchen and bathroom finishes and sanitaryware are all relatively easy to absorb in a factory production system. The issue around interfaces between materials for construction is that many of them are subject to legislation and regulation around structure, acoustics, fire and waterproofing. The current state-of-the-art in manufacturing in the UK is not currently able to be flexible on those elements in most cases. The future may very well be different.

Fig 13
Ijburg, Amsterdam, 2015

Urban House
Kidbrooke, London

FACTS

Location	Weigall Road, Greenwich, London, SE3 9FD
Planning authority	Royal Borough of Greenwich
Client	Berkeley Homes
Contractor	Berkeley Homes
Modular manufacturer	Elements Europe (2) and Caledonian (13)
Module construction	Steel frame
Architect	Berkeley Homes
Start date	2017
Completion date	2018
Number of homes	13
Number of modules	41
Storeys	3

The Berkeley Urban House is a three-storey terraced town house, designed for use on multiple sites alongside larger apartment buildings. The typology brings variety to the masterplan, and provides larger family accommodation at higher densities than is usually practical with individual houses. Their first use was as part of the Kidbrooke Village regeneration in Greenwich, with a total of 15 terraced houses. The typology has a simple rectangular footprint and is designed to be constructed back-to-back. The houses have no external rear garden, but provide a roof terrace across the entire roof. The terrace is accessed from a spiral stair on a small courtyard terrace on the first floor at the rear. Light for the rear of the first floor comes from a rooflight in the floor of the second-floor terrace. There is also a light funnel leading to the rear of the kitchen on the ground floor. The homes are designed to be delivered in three modules, with Caledonian Modular delivering the homes on Kidbrooke. It is likely that Berkeley Modular will supply these homes on future developments.

Fig 14
Urban House Kidbrooke,
Berkeley Homes, London
Borough of Greenwich, 2018

DIGITISING CUSTOM BUILD

In the Trevenson Park project HTA collaborated with the Potton custom-build timber-frame factory, part of the Kingspan Group. A range of house types were developed based on a standardised platform which could be customised for individual customers. On this particular project the aim was to offer customers a standardised plot for purchase, and to enable them to build a customised home on that plot. The master developer, Igloo, formed a panel of five manufacturers, each of whom worked with an architect to design a range of homes to fit on the standard plot and which offered a substantial amount of choice to the customer.

In parallel to this, HTA worked with Slider Studio on an InnovateUK funded research project to develop an online configuration tool which potential customers could use to investigate the customisation choices and options available to them.[13]

In deciding how much choice to offer customers, there is some tension between customer choice and prefabrication. The challenge lies in deciding the right balance to set between unlimited choice for the buyer and a level of prefabrication which is sensible for a manufacturing system to offer. Car, clothing and computer manufacturers have all pioneered systems to offer customisation where it is possible to offer choices that can be easily accommodated and manufactured. It is common practice when buying such goods to be offered a wide range of configuration choices to select from. Why can't housing offer the same?

It could be seen that this is a natural progression in housing design where the architect designs the set of choices, but the eventual customer makes the choice that suits them. It is likely that some manufacturers and clients will welcome this approach and embrace the restrictions that this approach brings in exchange for the benefits in quality control and cost reductions.

The planning system also has a role to play here, enabling choices, but not a free-for-all in terms of design quality or materials. There is no inherent contradiction between creating an attractive, well-planned place with good quality public realm and a consistent architectural language, while offering customer choices within a palette of materials and typologies.

Fig 15
Customisation options for a Kingspan Potton house type.

Heartlands, HTA Design LLP, Cornwall, 2016

Fig 16
A contemporary terraced house type for Urban Splash.

Irwell Riverside, shedkm, Manchester, 2019

Indeed some of the most successful and well-loved places to live are made of repetitive elements that are formed from the vernacular of the time and place, which creates identity from characteristics such as window sizes, materials or finishes.

CONCLUSION

There is no doubt that the new-build suburban family housing market in the UK is in desperate need of disruption.

The poor quality of much of the housing delivered by volume housebuilders dominating the market offers little choice to customers and obstructs new entrants into the market with higher quality aspirations. It is no surprise that the majority of home purchasers would prefer to buy an ageing second-hand, period home rather than a new one, because they value the spaciousness, better daylight and character on offer when compared to the cost driven standard product of the volume housebuilder, driven to the smallest practical rooms and windows through constant 'value-engineering'. However new developers, and the promise of more to come, are all seeking to harness the benefits of factory made construction to deliver housing that is spacious, well designed, flexible and with a high specification with lower embodied energy, and much reduced running costs, is to be welcomed. There are signs that we could be about to enter a new era in UK housebuilding where varied, flexible and customised designs are made available for purchase to a public stimulated by good quality domestic architecture.

CHAPTER 3
MAKING A MODULAR METROPOLIS

As the pace of urbanisation continues to accelerate around the world, our growing cities offer the chance to foster more sustainable patterns of living. To achieve such a goal, increasingly accepted as being essential to our future well-being and perhaps our very survival, we will need to forge a lower-carbon future within higher-performing buildings and within a greener, cleaner public realm.

Over the past decade modular construction has been shown to be particularly well suited to delivering greater urban intensification, enabling development on more compact, awkward and heavily constrained sites, with the significantly shorter construction period results in much less disruption for existing neighbours and the wider community. Starting the journey with the delivery of increasingly large and well considered hotels and student buildings, this form of construction has potentially found its future bedfellow in a convergence with the growing Build to Rent sector in the UK, with signs it may be equally suited to the smaller but growing co-living housing market. Indeed any form of living accommodation within a larger building owned, maintained and managed by a professional operator and institutional investor, is a prime candidate for harnessing the benefits of modular construction.

This chapter explores the factors that have driven this recent but rapid spurt in upward growth being delivered in the UK using modular prefabricated systems. We explore the technical challenges and benefits and the impact on investment that has partly driven the market so rapidly. This chapter also details the multiple benefits realised directly from modular prefabrication to construction and to the economic, social and environmental outcomes of the project and asks, 'what are the upper limitations of our emerging modular metropolis?'

'Modular building need not be different from the practice followed in Edinburgh New Town and Notting Hill Gate.'
The report of the **Building Better, Building Beautiful Commission**[1]

Facing page
Mapleton Crescent,
Metropolitan Workshop, London
Borough of Wandsworth, 2019

A SHORT HISTORY OF URBAN MODULAR LIVING

The rise of urban modular buildings started with something of a false dawn at the turn of the 20th century with a number of projects by Peabody Trust which sought to speed up the delivery of homes, with fewer defects and lower costs, by investing in the use of volumetric modular construction. The two most notable projects, both in Hackney, were Murray Grove which is covered as a case study in Chapter 1, and Raines Court completed in 2003 and described in more detail here. By 2007 Caledonian had taken modular structures up to 17 storeys with the Paragon development in Brentford for Berkeley First, soon followed by an even taller student housing scheme, the 25-storey Liberty Heights in Wolverhampton, the first UK scheme completed by Vision Modular Systems. Although quite different in form, scale and appearance all were characterised by a keenness by the designers to express the form of construction within. Although potentially considered an honest expression of the building form, it is at odds with the visual appearance of most other forms of construction.

The first major modular building to be commissioned after the recession of 2008 was Shubette House in Wembley. Combining a complex mix of uses the proposed scheme included a hotel, private and affordable housing above retail. It was driven by quite specific requirements of the planners that were to test the versatility of the system, and this project set a significant precedent for the creative possibilities of future modular projects.

Meanwhile across the Atlantic, 461 Dean Street in Brooklyn was breaking new heights with a 32-storey modular tower (featured in Chapter 6) though not without some challenges in terms of the difficult relationship between manufacturer and developer.

Notwithstanding the progress made over the past decade in scaling new heights in urban modular buildings across London in particular, delivery has been driven by a relatively small number of companies. It seems likely that the market will continue to expand with new manufacturers entering in response to increasing demand from institutionally funded investors within the rental sector, including Build to Rent, student and co-living housing.

Raines Court
Hackney, London

FACTS

Location	Northwold Road, Hackney, London, N16 7DG
Planning authority	London Borough of Hackney
Client	Peabody Trust
Contractor	Wates
Modular manufacturer	Yorkon
Module construction	Light steel frame
Architect	Allford Hall Monaghan Morris
Start date	1999
Completion date	2003
Construction period	23 months
Number of homes	52 shared ownership, 8 private sale
Number of modules	127
Site area	0.3 hectares

Fig 1
Raines Court stands as the first Housing Corporation funded modular housing scheme in the country.

Raines Court, AHMM, London Borough of Hackney, 2003

Peabody continued their investment in modular housing, completing a scheme of 53 apartments and eight additional private sale live/work spaces within a six-storey building at Raines Court in Stoke Newington. Designed by Allford Hall Monaghan Morris the project aimed to refine the manufacturing and assembly process and as a result was able to reduce the average number of modules required per apartment from an average of three to two, with each module measuring 4.2x18m, the maximum size for more efficient delivery and installation. Further innovations included the incorporation of recessed balconies within the modules that enabled internal and external spaces to be offset or staggered, helping to enliven the elevation, while modules were also delivered part clad to further reduce finishing on site. As at Murray Grove, the building very much expresses the modular construction although here the cladding seeks a more continuous expression with horizontal and vertical banding to each module junction and uses a different material to express the traditionally built core.

The upper level apartments are accessed by a deck fixed to the north side of the building which not only suits the southerly aspect of the living rooms but also strengthens the street frontage. Both the two- and three-bed apartments make use of the deck and private balconies to provide multiple means of escape and enable an incredibly efficient internal layout with minimal circulation space, again in part driven by the aspiration to minimise the number of modules for greater efficiency. The module width also enabled every room in each apartment to be fully contained within a single module, avoiding complex 'zipping up' of rooms spanning between modules.

One of the more significant aspects of the development was its shared ownership tenure, with all 53 homes part sold, with no reported problems of securing mortgages, and proving that such innovation need not be limited to the rental market. Post-occupancy feedback by Peabody found high levels of satisfaction with the homes, in terms of both design and the quality of finish, and the majority of residents expressed a positive view of the construction method with some even citing this as a reason for buying there. Some 16 years after occupation the building continues to look in great condition and well cared for.

Fig 2
South facing covered balconies.

Raines Court, AHMM, London Borough of Hackney, 2003

THE MANUFACTURERS

VISION MODULAR SYSTEMS

Having developed a number of buildings in Ireland, Vision Modular Systems, working with sister company Tide Construction, a developer/contractor, emerged as sector leaders in their fully integrated business model that has enabled rapid delivery of ever more complex projects including the current tallest modular building in the world in Croydon (101 George Street) and a wide range of building forms and housing types. As a result of their prolific output there are no fewer than eight Vision buildings included within this book. Vision are particularly notable for the level of investment in R&D to demonstrate the technical robustness and long-term sustainability of their projects.

ELEMENTS EUROPE

Until relatively recently Elements Europe focused on relative low- and mid-rise hotels but over the past few years have developed their expertise delivering a stylish Build to Rent tower for Essential Living at Union Wharf in Greenwich (see case study 6) while work is also underway to deliver the 20-storey Addiscombe Grove, also in Croydon, for Pocket Living.

Elements have recently confirmed significant investment in their production facility from GS&EC, a large Korean contractor/developer which is expected to enable them to expand their factory capacity and carry out more R&D into construction methodology. It is likely that this will also lead to technical know-how flowing into Asia where there are significant markets for modular construction.

CALEDONIAN MODULAR

Caledonian Modular have a long history of delivering successful modular projects across multiple sectors including education, healthcare, military, hotels and housing. More recently they have been focusing on expanding their housing provision and looking again to deliver at greater scale having completed temporary accommodation for workers at the Hinkley Point power station.

BERKELEY MODULAR

Already a major housebuilder, Berkeley is working across London and the south-east with the benefit of a significant pipeline of housing from the many sites the group has under development. Investment in a factory and production machinery is already underway and it is expected that the first prototype modular homes will arrive in early 2021.

INTERNATIONAL EXPERTISE

As modular construction is increasingly accepted and even welcomed in the UK as a positive way to deliver more homes, to a higher quality and at higher densities, while delivering more energy efficient housing, more international companies are entering the market. These include companies such as Polcom from Poland, Forta PRO from Latvia and CIMC from China, all currently delivering housing projects in the UK. Providing the economics of transportation logistics are able to be sustained as Europe changes post-Brexit, it seems likely that there will be no shortage of customers for their expertise should they continue to deliver successful outcomes.

Shubette House
Wembley, London

FACTS

Location	5 Olympic Way, Wembley, London, HA9 0NS
Planning authority	London Borough of Brent
Client	Pinnacle
Contractor	Tide Construction Ltd
Modular manufacturer	Vision Modular Systems
Module construction	Steel frame and concrete slab hybrid
Architect	HTA Design LLP
Start date	2009
Completion date	2013
Construction period	18 months
Number of homes	158 homes, 237 hotel/apart hotel rooms
Number of modules	831
Storeys	11-20

Designed and delivered either side of the financial crash and great recession of 2008-10, this project provided an early indication of the new potential of the next generation of modular housing. A mixed use development incorporates a hotel and apart hotel, a residential tower of 20 storeys with lower connecting blocks above ground floor retail units, and a basement car park. The buildings wrap around a courtyard that combines provision of resident amenity space and coach parking, all sitting above a basement car park. This complex programme, the array of site constraints and the required flexibility of built form not normally associated with repetitive modular construction. Indeed the project forms a case study in the potential of advanced modular systems to deliver the variety and creativity usually required in the development of constrained urban sites, where it is not practical for the massing and expression of the building to be overly constrained by the limitations of a particular system. The architecture seeks to express the precision engineering of the modular manufacturing without expressing the individual modules. The curved form of the tower is made possible by wrapping the tower form in a balcony framework which also provided the working platform for the cladding of the tower.

The reinforced *in-situ* concrete superstructure basement and ground floor provides a transfer slab at first floor level of almost a metre thick, with five separate cores rising above.

A plan of a typical floor shows the huge variety of module shapes and sizes required to deliver the varied accommodation types and housing mix. Due to a late change in the tower location requested by the Brent planners, there is even a transition between modules spanning perpendicular to each other between lower and upper floors. Although always designed with modular construction in mind, the need to respond to the development viability dictated some extraordinary complexity, all delivered according to the original budget.

Planning permission was secured in June 2009, with construction starting in late 2011 and completing 18 months later in early 2013.

The housing delivers a mix of private, affordable rented and shared ownership homes, and although originally designed for private sale, the tower was purchased for management as specialist private rented housing with additional amenities added in an early signal of this sector's appreciation of the benefits of modular construction. It has been fully occupied since 2013, and a visit to the hotel provides evidence of the robustness and longevity of the modular system.

Fig 3
Terracotta bay windows on hotel facade facing Wembley Stadium

THE METRICS OF THE MODULAR APARTMENT

As we did in Chapter 2 in relation to the typical family house, it is important to understand the dimensional drivers guiding the design of apartments. In some respects matters are much more straightforward but there are also some crucial challenges to overcome.

As with family houses the challenge is to enclose whole rooms within individual modules to minimise connections on site and enable high-quality installations and finishing to be factory based. As before, the width is an important limitation but with most bedrooms typically ranging between 2.85m and 3.2m wide, and living rooms having a minimum width of 3.5m, but rarely rising above 3.8m, with enclosing walls this keeps overall module widths below 4m, ideal for transportation in more crowded urban areas. Contrary to popular misconception, most manufacturers do not limit production to any shape, providing it's a rectangle. Indeed various plans included throughout this book and particularly within the case studies in Part II, demonstrate the huge variety that most manufacturers can achieve.

This highlights one of the challenges facing modular manufacturers. Unlike in suburban housing where standardisation with elements of customisation is the target, the urban apartment block requires a bespoke response to ensure the development is optimised for viability whatever the shape of the site, the constraints from neighbouring buildings or the expectations of the local planning department.

As a result the more successful modular manufacturers have become those that are both able to adapt the system to deliver maximum variety, while of course noting that by and large, most homes are based on fairly regular rectangular shapes.

A METHODOLOGY FOR MODULARISATION

As the benefits of modular delivery become increasingly apparent, buildings designed for traditional construction are being converted for modular delivery. This can provide plenty of challenges and early analysis is needed by an architect experienced in the proposed system to assess whether a quick conversion is possible or whether a revision of the design would better enable more rapid production and assembly and still bring programme savings. Based on the metrics set out above and the flexibility offered by most manufacturers specialising in high-rise modular the conversion process can be quite straightforward. Buildings and apartments based around well-considered sensible layouts with well-proportioned rooms should provide no obstacles. Figure 4 is a demonstration of the conversion from traditional to modular build of a typical two-bedroom flat at Tillermans, Greenford Quay. Rooms maintained similar widths, and minor amendments were in part due to the client's design development. Perhaps more revealing was that despite the introduction of double partitions between rooms (itself providing added sound separation) the overall area of the apartment increased, due to increased efficiencies in the dimensions of party and external walls.

There are a few key principles that the designer should adhere to and recognise. The structure and services should align vertically. Whether building traditionally or using modular, this is a sensible starting point. Ideally modular rooms would form completely enclosed spaces, minimising the need for onsite work within the module.

Not all materials and systems behave in the same way, and there are differences between the performance and thickness of different materials used in modular construction. Some materials such as hot-rolled steel and precast concrete are appropriate for very high-

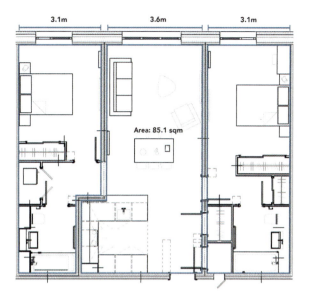

Fig 4
Comparison of a typical two-bed apartment, before and after modularisation.

Greenford Quay, HTA Design LLP, London Borough of Ealing, 2016

Fig 5
Modular design principles – the major elements of the building structure, infill walls, and service elements combined together to form a single volumetric module

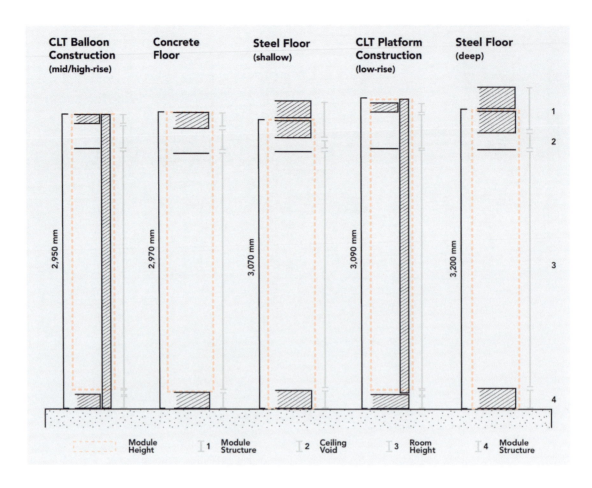

Fig 6
The impact of materials on module heights

rise buildings, others are suitable for lower rise, such as light-gauge steel and timber frames. The choice of system and material has an impact on the overall size of the building. If the building height is limited, then a shallower floor system will offer advantages.

It helps to think of the building as a 'kit of parts' which when assembled will form the final structure. The size of each element and how it can be transported and delivered matters a great deal. How each element relates to the other elements needs to be considered as well as how each component is fixed to the other and in what sequence.

There is a typical installation sequence of a building composed of steel-framed modules which is a little different from a timber-framed one and quite different to a precast concrete one. The characteristics of each system need to be understood by the architect in advance of designing the details of the building to ensure that the installation sequence is workable, safe and delivers a robust structure.

MAKING A MODULAR METROPOLIS

Vertical Stacking

1. Ensure structural elements stack vertically
2. Ensure services stack vertically
3. Aim to stack similar unit types, but there can be exceptions

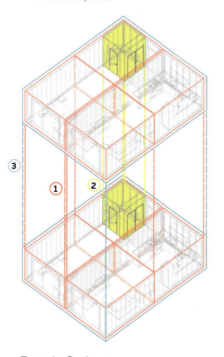

Double Wall conditions at module junctions

1. Allow for double wall widths at module junctions
2. Use doors or larger openings to conceal joints between modules

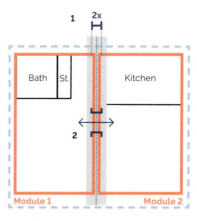

Indicative
One Bedroom Unit

Facade Options

Fully finishing the facades in the factory can greatly reduce time on site, but will require forward thinking, and care by those involved to retain the condition of the finishes, and conceal final joints between modules

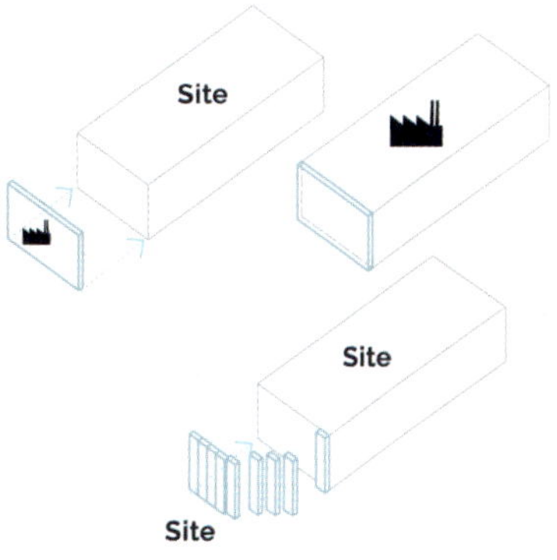

Modular Installation Sequence

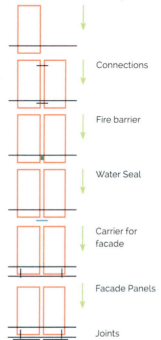

Fig 7 (top left)
Vertical Stacking

Fig 8 (top right)
Double Wall conditions

Fig 9 (bottom left)
Facade Options – prefabricate the facade in the factory and install on-site, prefabricate in the factory and install in the factory or manufacture on site and install on site

Fig 10 (bottom right)
Modular Installation Sequence – the steps taken to install a module and integrate it into the building fabric

PREFABRICATION BENEFITS FOR URBAN HIGH-RISE

There are significant benefits in the choice of large modular prefabrication as the method for delivery of urban high-rise residential projects, as the case studies illustrate in Part II. These benefits span many aspects of the projects, particularly socio-economic and environmental.

The benefits to the project are realised as the building is finished to a high standard of quality in approximately half the time it takes for a comparable building to be constructed using traditional methods.[2] In this way, the design team have finished their work sooner and can move on to another project, and similarly the client and construction teams can also move on to other projects, so everyone involved is at least twice as productive than in traditional construction. For architects, this means that once a building is detailed and designed, the team is free to move on to another project as the manufacturing process means that there is no opportunity for further value-engineering or changes in design. The requirement for site supervision is reduced to the common areas, cladding, external works and the roof. The internal fit-outs of the rooms are likely to be snag-free. If they aren't, then there is a change needed in the design or manufacturing process on the next project.

Fig 11
A module being lifted into place at Holloway Road, delivered by Tide Construction Ltd & Vision Modular Systems.

Chapter Highbury II, HTA Design LLP, London Borough of Islington, 2017

Fig 12
A module being lifted into place. Note Tide Construction's lifting frame ensuring that the module is lifted vertically and no horizontal loads are placed on the module structure.

George Street, HTA Design LLP, London Borough of Croydon, 2019

Offsite modular construction makes particular sense in urban areas, as the site becomes easier to manage. Tight urban sites are often characterised by restrictions on how much space a contractor has available to use for storage of materials, site facilities, canteens, rest rooms and staff offices. Moving tasks into a factory means that the site is left clear for the contractor to start construction with fewer constraints and moving the bulk of the workforce into a factory also means that the need for on-site accommodation is reduced to a minimum.

Large-scale prefabricated elements such as volumetric modules can also be delivered to a site at times that suit the local planning authority, with the aid of a coordinated manufacturer and supply chain. Typically, several trucks deliver modules overnight and these are parked in a buffer area near to the site. The modules are then delivered in the correct sequence to the site and installed onto the building using a suitable tower crane. Due to the weight of the modules, sometimes in excess of 20 tonnes, a large fixed tower crane is usually required (precast concrete modules can be significantly heavier). It takes between 30 minutes and one hour to install and fix each module into place, which means that a rate of installation of seven to eight modules per day is common. This is not the maximum installation rate as it can be increased if multiple cranes are used or if there is a skilled installation team working on a repetitive project.

Each module can be up to 5m wide and 18m long, meaning that a one-person apartment can be delivered in a pair of modules, a two-bedroom apartment in three modules, and a three-bedroom apartment in four. Assuming that eight modules are delivered per day, five days per week, a week of module installations can deliver 20 one-bedroom apartments or 10 three-bedroom apartments. The number of deliveries and the speed of installation depend on the capacity of the factory to supply modules to site at the desired speed and frequency.

With this speed of delivery and quality, given that each module is largely finished internally, it demonstrates that large-scale projects can be delivered faster than with traditional construction while factory based finishing enables a higher standard of finish.[3]

It is important to identify the crane position relatively early on during construction, to ensure that the crane is installed in the right location to be able to deliver the heavy modules to all points of the building, and to ascertain whether if one crane is insufficient, a second crane is needed or if it is better to build in sections. For particularly tight sites the crane can be installed on the core, if the core is suitably strengthened to take the extra loads, but this requires an additional temporary crane to install the main crane and then a secondary crane to remove it at the end of the process.

MODULAR AIRSPACE

Meanwhile, some other developers are seeking to adopt modular solutions to meet their individual business needs without becoming manufacturers themselves, by purchasing modules from manufacturers already available on the market. Companies such as Apex Airspace and Fruition Properties who are seeking to add additional floors on top of existing buildings using modular extensions are currently active across London, though the model is relatively untested to date.

Fig 13
Apex Airspace rooftop development.

Antony & Roderick, HTA Design LLP, London Borough of Southwark, 2019

MAKING A MODULAR METROPOLIS

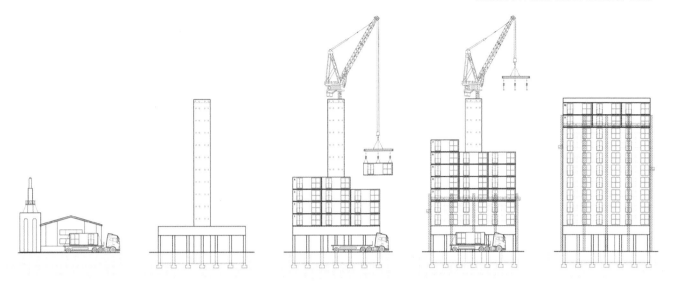

Fig 14
HTA diagram of the modular construction process in five stages

1. Factory Production and Site Construction start together
2. Site Construction of Core and Podium while modules are manufactured
3. Module installation begins
4. Facade installation begins
5. Facade and internal fit-out completes

DEALING WITH CONSTRAINED SITES

Some UK projects where large-scale prefabrication has been used in recent years are sites where there was a significant challenge to the use of traditional construction. Examples include sites where there is restricted access, for example near to railway lines or busy junctions; sites where the building uses up most if not all of the site (see case studies on Mapleton Crescent and George Street, Croydon); sites where deliveries can only happen outside of normal working hours and sites where there are difficult ground conditions which limit the size and scale of the building. The CitizenM hotel above Tower Hill underground station is a good example where extra storeys were added because modular construction is typically lighter than traditional *in-situ* reinforced concrete.

The socio-economic benefits of prefabrication also come from reducing construction time and from eliminating many on-site construction tasks. The lives of those surrounding the building sites are less affected by the construction than if the project were to be built traditionally because the construction period is halved. There is less disruption in the immediate area also because there are far fewer people and vehicle movements required than in a traditional delivery method. There is less noise from the construction, little or no dust and hardly any heavy plant on site.

Other social benefits to be realised from offsite construction are to the workers themselves. Generally, having a fixed employment location – the factory – enables a healthier lifestyle than a changing location, as happens for on-site workers who generally need to commute to different sites every morning. Working at a fixed address offers construction staff a regular commute which they can choose to shorten by moving closer to the factory, perhaps even close enough to cycle or walk to work. Furthermore, they can have a standard working day which can provide a better work-life balance.

Better education and skill levels required to work at a prefabrication factory versus traditional on-site construction also form an important socio-economic benefit of the growing modular prefabrication construction method. As people who work in factories are closely managed and trained, construction-related accidents can be reduced, making these jobs safer. People who would not have considered a job in construction may become more attracted by the sector for future employment, as it can mean a safer, cleaner and more accessible job. This may enable a more diverse workforce in factory-based construction-sector jobs in the future.

Bollo Lane
Ealing, London

FACTS

Location	100 Bollo Lane, London, W4 5LX
Planning authority	London Borough of Ealing
Client	Pocket Living
Contractor	Tide Construction Ltd
Modular manufacturer	Vision Modular Systems
Module construction	Steel frame and concrete slab hybrid
Architect	PRP
Start date	July 2017
Completion date	July 2019
Construction period	24 months
Number of homes	84 Pocket Homes and 28 private for sale homes
Number of modules	260
Storeys	13

100 Bollo Lane is one of three projects within this book by Pocket Living, a London-based developer specialising in smaller one-bedroom apartments for first-time buyers.

The scheme includes 84 'Pocket' discounted sale affordable homes, along with 28 private sale apartments to provide some cross subsidy to help fund the development along with some flexible office space. In common with quite a few of the urban projects studied here the site is characterised by complex constraints, with three separate railway lines passing the edge of the site on three sides. Designed by PRP the project was delivered by Vision Modular Systems, who had already completed a number of projects for Pocket.

Fig 15
A landmark building delivered on a constraint site.

100 Bollo Lane, PRP, London Borough of Ealing, 2019

SUSTAINABILITY BENEFITS

There are many environmental benefits to the use of modular construction, but some are not as obvious as others or as well researched and understood. More work needs to be done to understand the environmental impact of factory production and the path to decarbonising construction. Some work carried out by Heriot-Watt University makes a direct comparison between traditional and volumetric construction for the same building and indicates a substantial benefit across all indicators, including a halving of the embodied energy in the building.

This radar diagram (see Figure 14) illustrates the environmental impact of a traditional build approach (blue) compared to the lesser impact of a volumetric modular approach (orange). This is measured against a typical spectrum of environmental indicators typically used in life cycle assessment analysis (LCA).

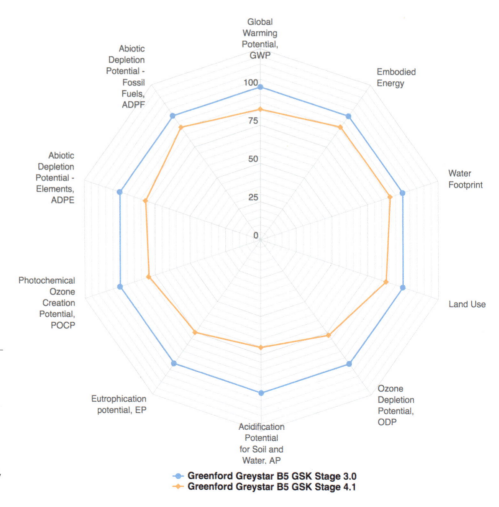

Fig 16
Research by Heriot-Watt showing the comparison of modular and conventional construction using 10 environmental indicators.

Greenford Quay, HTA Design LLP, London Borough of Ealing, 2016

Fig 17
Interiors views of the build to rent residential amenities for Greystar, delivered by Tide Construction Ltd.

Greenford Quay, HTA Design LLP, London Borough of Ealing, 2019

The performance of the building when finished is higher than if delivered using traditional construction as the quality control over the construction work in the factory is better than that on a building site.[4] The well-documented 'performance gap' that is prevalent in traditional construction is much less likely in factory-based construction as every element of the building constructed in the factory is subject to a high level of quality assurance. A good illustration of this is that tolerance levels of 1mm height or length over several floors are typical of modular construction, which is unheard of in traditional construction where 10–15mm is more usual. Furthermore, working on the factory floor is safer, with convenient access to tools and materials, and with better supervision helping to maintain consistent quality control.

Typically, a prefabricated module is composed of elements that are tagged on entry to the factory and the module is then tracked through the stages of manufacture and finishing through to completion and exiting the factory. A complete audit trail will be available showing who worked on the module, when it was done, who supervised it and who assessed it as completed. Some building control organisations send their teams to audit the factory processes as part of their work, as some processes cannot be easily checked on site, realising that such checks bring confidence to the industry that prefabrication is a better way to deliver high-quality buildings.

However, current environmental legislation does not recognise the benefits of prefabrication, as many of these benefits, such as the lower embodied energy used to deliver the building, are not taken into account in any current planning guidance or UK regulation. As the construction industry moves to decarbonise its activities it is essential that innovation continues in how buildings are delivered, to remove or mitigate the environmental impact of a building at construction stage. Using prefabrication is a great start and, depending on the material used, it can reduce the environmental impact substantially. It is noticeable that the commonly used environmental rating systems for buildings such as BREEAM, LEED, etc., do not specifically mention prefabrication as a desirable methodology for environmental improvement. This is a regulatory gap, as the benefits to the industry, to society and to the environment from constructing high-quality buildings through the fast prefabrication of large modular designs is enormous. While rating systems ignore this they are missing out on supporting a good way to deliver the benefits that environmental rating systems have been set up to address.

Watts Grove
Tower Hamlets, London

FACTS

Location	Watts Grove, Tower Hamlets, London, E3 3UU
Planning authority	London Borough of Tower Hamlets
Client	Swan NU Living
Contractor	Swan NU Build
Modular manufacturer	Swan NU Living
Module construction	Cross laminated timber (CLT)
Architect	Waugh Thistleton
Start date	2019
Completion date	2020
Construction period	c. 12 months
Number of homes	65
Storeys	6

Watts Grove is the UK's first mid-rise modular cross laminated timber (CLT) scheme in the UK, in Bow Common, east London. Designed by CLT specialists Waugh Thistleton and built for affordable housing provider Swan Housing Association, the homes are manufactured from sustainably forested CLT and assembled into modules at Swan NU Living's factory in Basildon ready for delivery to site.

The modules are delivered fully finished with kitchens and bathrooms installed, to benefit from enhanced quality control, and the construction programme is expected to be 50% shorter than a traditional build and at 10% less cost. Furthermore, relative to a comparable building in traditional construction, the 2,350sqm of CLT within the structure will lock away 1857 tonnes of CO_2, with the building functioning as a carbon store.

Notwithstanding the pioneering nature of this project, the future has become more uncertain for mid-rise CLT construction. Recent changes to building regulations arising from concern about combustibility risk undermining the contribution CLT can make to creating healthy buildings and a low carbon future.

Figs 18, 19
Modules are assembled at Swan's factory in Basildon using sustainably forested CLT.

Watts Grove, Waugh Thistleton, London Borough of Tower Hamlets, 2020

FORM FOLLOWS FINANCE

Large UK construction projects are increasingly seen as safe and desirable investments for both national and overseas investors, providing higher stable returns. Property prices in the British residential sector have continuously risen for many decades, as the lack of housing supply and the challenges to delivery continue to increase prices for both sale and rental properties.[5]

However, UK construction costs using traditional construction methods have also grown by 2-4% per annum in urban areas over the last decade.[6] Construction productivity has lagged behind, leaving clients getting less for their money but having to pay more. Meanwhile, manufacturing productivity worldwide continues to grow, demonstrating the continuing benefits to be gained from investing in manufacturing.

This is attributed to several issues affecting construction in general, such as a lack of productivity in traditional contracting, skills shortages, wage growth due to inflation and a shrinking workforce.[7] In addition, increasingly demanding regulations on thermal performance, safety, pollution and environmental performance are contributing to increased costs;[8] and while dense urban sites suitable for tall buildings are where higher returns can be made, they have additional risks such as the problems of traffic, phasing and site management, which also add to this growing bill.

When these issues are considered in the round it has become common for investors to look for alternative, more cost-efficient ways to deliver these large projects by means of tackling the inefficiency of traditional construction and reducing on-site management issues. The key to investment returns in large complex construction projects is to guarantee the timeframe for delivering the building, and investors are focused on reducing any risks that add on-site complexity or uncertainty which can delay the project. For this reason,

Fig 20
Growth in construction and manufacturing sector compared to the whole economy

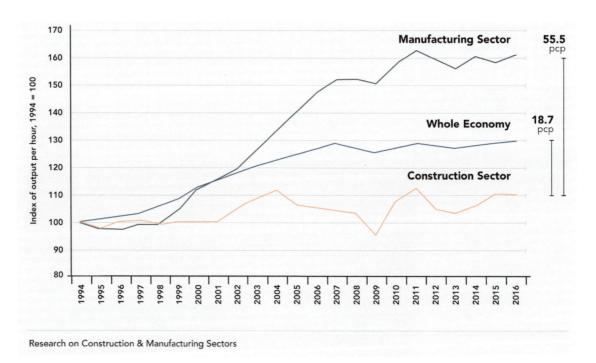

Research on Construction & Manufacturing Sectors

investors are increasingly likely to take a more active role in ensuring that a project is delivered on time by influencing the actual methodology for delivery, for example investing in processes to help construct buildings, as well as on tools to analyse risk and construction methodology.

In recent years, an investor's approach to tackle inefficiencies from traditional construction has widened to include large-scale modular factory production. This is particularly suited to delivering high-rise urban projects based on a design that maximises modularisation in the building, as has been demonstrated for many years in hotels and student buildings that have been successfully delivered in the UK and elsewhere. The link between offsite production and a quick and guaranteed delivery of a building, with high-quality finishes and on budget has been obvious to investors in non-residential markets for over a decade, and it is now expanding to the residential sector.[9]

In the past, investors have gone even further, taking more control over the delivery methodology and have set up factories. For example, one student developer, Unite, set up its own modular factory in 2002 to deliver student housing for its own ownership, and built a number of buildings that it still owns. A change of management direction and challenging markets led to the factory closure in 2011, but nevertheless this venture demonstrated the benefits of joined up investment, development and manufacturing. It also highlighted the difficulties of factory ownership and management, and the problems of using a factory that has a continuous overhead which exists whether there is work for it in the pipeline or not. A development business must be of a sufficient scale to provide enough demand to keep a factory busy, or the model won't work. Currently a number of investors in the UK are either working on their plans for new factories or are even more advanced in their decision-making and have already set up a factory for production of prefabricated modules for their residential projects.

Fig 21
Union Wharf for Essential Living with Elements Europe as the modular manufacturers.

Union Wharf, Assael Architecture & HTA Design LLP, Greenwich, 2019

Fig 22
Two 40-storey concrete volumetric modular towers constructed by Dragages Singapore.

Clement Canopy, ADDP Architects, Singapore, 2019

Other investors in the residential market who chose not to set up their own factory are still choosing to pursue modular construction systems fabricated offsite and are content to buy products from a variety of manufacturers, providing that they can meet their demanding specifications. Examples of this approach in the current UK market include 3M providing investment funding to Essential Living for the construction of Greenwich Creekside, a 21-storey modular apartment building for rent and Canadian Pension Ivanhoe providing funding to Greystar for the construction of Greenford Quay, a 1,950-home development for private sale and private rental buildings ranging from seven to 17 storeys in Ealing, London, as well as 101 George Street, a 46- and 38-storey private rental building of 546 apartments in Croydon, London. The scale of these projects demonstrates that investors are increasingly confident that large-scale prefabrication brings significant benefits and are willing to fund factories so that their high-rise urban projects can make use of it.

SCALING NEW MODULAR HEIGHTS

The current direction of modular prefabrication appears to be up! For many years modular suppliers have concentrated on low-rise buildings, schools, healthcare facilities and temporary accommodation. The current demand from projects and designers includes a large number of tall buildings in dense urban locations around the world, fuelled by demand for housing, as discussed for the UK earlier, and for other denser cities worldwide. Hong Kong and Singapore are both driving their construction industries towards using more prefabrication, calling it modular integrated construction (MIC) in Hong Kong and prefinished prefabricated volumetric construction (PPVC) in Singapore. In the case study on Clement Canopy (see page 199), a 40-storey modular concrete building in Singapore demonstrates the progress that is possible in a few short years in a country that has only recently adopted this approach. In the UK the construction of the 44-storey project at 101 George Street, Croydon, has opened up the question of how high modular can go.

For architects this presents challenges and opportunities. For a tall building built using volumetric construction it needs to be designed this way from the outset, and the designer needs to satisfy themselves that the project is appropriate for the approach at an early stage and that there is appetite among the client and delivery team to take that direction. Involving a manufacturer at an early design stage is to be recommended as well as an engineer that is fully confident in the design of tall structures built this way. Some issues are in the early stages of research and are relatively untested, such as the behaviour of a tall modular building in high winds, but each new building constructed brings an opportunity for knowledge and study.

CONCLUSION

With a growing collection of perhaps 20 residential buildings in complex urban sites delivered using modular construction, London is currently leading the modular way for the rest of the world. Amongst these various projects are showcases for quality of design, speed of delivery, innovation in manufacture and more sustainable production though reduced energy, waste and embodied carbon. Modular construction has created an estimated 12,000 homes for Londoners in the past decade, and at an accelerating rate.

High-rise modular construction: An engineer's perspective

Michael Hough, MJH Structural

Tall volumetric modular construction offers a manufactured solution to an industry where supply cannot meet demand and where this difficulty is escalating. Modular construction has been used for various heights of buildings but offers the most benefits for mid- to high-rise construction, where many of the benefits exceed traditional construction methods. The speed of delivery of the completed building, reducing uncertainties, together with large elements of the building lifted into place with internal finishes completed makes this method of construction the most efficient way to deliver tall construction.

Based on our one group of designers and builders and the distance that we have travelled with this modular system in a short number of years it would be very presumptuous to put a limiting height on what may be achieved in the next few years. It is very likely that the limitation to the height of current modular construction will be related to building elements that are non-modular by nature and may be increased as time goes by and further research informs our understanding.

Fig 23
Installation of the glazed terracotta cladding delivered by Tide Construction Ltd.

George Street, HTA Design LLP, London Borough of Croydon, 2020

Investors have been helping to fund factories while governments in the UK and elsewhere are actively promoting this method of construction to help speed up project delivery, and improve certainty of delivery, with the expectation that a more mature market would ultimately drive down costs.

For dense urban cities around the world, many with a housing crisis of their own to tackle, there are many lessons to be learned, and plenty of expertise for the UK to export, for investors in new forms of housing within buildings that they will own, manage and maintain for the long term there are numerous examples to learn from.

There is now growing evidence available to measure quite empirically how adopting offsite construction methods brings additional benefits to the project, to the on-site team, and to neighbours in the immediate construction area, as well as to society and to the environment in the form of pollution and emission reductions.

The case studies featured in this book demonstrate that volumetric modular prefabrication is a force for positive change within the housing industry with a bright future ahead.

CHAPTER 4
ARCHITECTS AS DESIGNERS IN INDUSTRY

Could architects describe their role as being 'designers in industry', while working closely with manufacturing and prefabrication? This could be a statement of determination to be a core part of the manufacturing process and not simply a 'user' or 'consumer' of it. There is the potential for architects to act in a similar way to some of the designers in recent industrial history, who developed a crucial understanding of manufacturing in a period of change and used that knowledge to develop designs that were attractive, functional and successful. Some of the references for this type of design understanding come from the car industry where there is a long history of designers working closely with manufacturers to produce cars that were substantially better than the competition due to breakthroughs in material science, technology, manufacturing or design ingenuity. For example, André Lefèbvre knew how to manufacture cars using lightweight materials, and the Citroën 2CV demonstrates this knowledge by being the lightest car on the market, using the smallest amount of materials. The Citroën DS introduced a host of innovations, from hydro-pneumatic suspension to headlights that turned with the car as it cornered. At around the same time, Alec Issigonis launched his design for the original Mini, turning the engine sideways to create more space, and revolutionised small car design.

> 'Houses are NOT cars: houses have an orientation, they enclose space, they form streetscapes, they have to last a long time, but crucially, they don't have any certainty of demand. Is this what makes the notion of housing as a production line so alien – and perhaps unrealistic?'
>
> **Claire Bennie**, Municipal

Facing page
Chapter White City, HTA Design LLP, London Borough of Hammersmith & Fulham, 2018

Fig 1
The iconic design of the Mini, regularly voted as the most influential car of the 20th century after the Ford Model T

Fig 2
The Citroën 2CV

These, and all of the best car designers not only possess the creative talents to shape and style their products, but also an understanding of engineering that enables their creations to function brilliantly as well be beautiful. The designer is central to the process, but thoroughly immersed in the industry so as to be part of the team needed to deliver excellence. They frequented the factories and spoke to the teams who manufactured components. They spent time in the showrooms discussing the marketing of the vehicles and understood what customers wanted, working closely with scientists and researchers who had made breakthroughs in their research into materials, aerodynamics and performance of engines and other components. This detailed knowledge enabled them to connect these specialist developments and to link them through innovative designs that were popular with the market. The role of the architect in modern housing manufacture is comparable. It brings the architect back into the core of the design and manufacturing process and at the heart of the decision-making.

UNDERSTANDING THE MATERIAL

The history of 20th-century architecture is packed with innovations from leading architects, experimenting in housing design and production, considered to be one of the most important areas of architectural enquiry.

Frank Lloyd Wright understood the cantilever better than his contemporaries and used it in his seminal design of Fallingwater. He famously removed the supports to the cantilevered terraces because the contractor was afraid to. Louis Kahn tried to think clearly about the nature of materials and how they can be used in a way that suits their inherent properties. His well-known challenge to his students of architecture, to 'ask the brick what it wants to be', is an enigmatic request of his students to understand the material they were designing with and to use it effectively.[1] This is a request that still resonates today and is probably more urgent than ever as environmental concerns demand that we use materials sparingly and eliminate waste. Both Kahn and Lloyd Wright understood that materials have capabilities that matter and by focusing on their inherent qualities good architecture can be created economically, rather than focusing on appearance first and then finding a means to achieve that appearance that involves complex and expensive compromises.

ARCHITECTS AS DESIGNERS IN INDUSTRY

Fig 3
The design relies on the pioneering use of cantilevers to achieve its aim of projecting the inhabitant into the landscape.

Fallingwater, Frank Lloyd Wright, Pennsylvania, 1935

Fig 4
A seminal work of repetition and standardisation in a then-modern material.

Unité d'Habitation, Le Corbusier, Marseille, France, 1952

Le Corbusier understood the properties and potential of reinforced concrete so well that when coupled with his astonishingly original thinking he produced artful masterpieces such as Ronchamp, and a whole town in a building – the Unité d'habitation in Marseille, where the plastic nature of concrete enabled the designer to produce a poetic and functional structure,

THE GENESIS OF MANUFACTURED HOUSING

Others were to investigate the potential of mass-produced housing through the design of individual homes. French engineer and architect Jean Prouvé understood the nature of steel and how to assemble it better than his contemporaries which led to him designing steel components, products, furniture, and building systems including a type of brise soleil that could be considered a forerunner of modern mass-produced systems. He is probably best known for his *pièce de résistance*, a prefabricated steel-framed housing typology for Africa. This was conceived with a steel structure designed to be light enough to be delivered by air.

Fig 5
A prefabricated design for the tropics developed to be delivered by air and therefore made from the lightest materials available.

Maison Tropicale, Jean Prouvé, France, 2008

Fig 6
Eames House, Charles and Ray Eames, Los Angeles, 2013

The Packaged House[2] by Konrad Wachsmann and Walter Gropius was a house that could be constructed in less than nine hours and proposed a number of ideas around mass production, while the Dymaxion House by Buckminster Fuller was a homage to the car manufacturers driving innovation in mid-century USA with various prototypes developed for factory manufacture. In the late 1940s Charles and Ray Eames built the Eames House in California, a prototype for customised housing built from standard components readily available from the builders' merchant.

Towards the end of the 20th century a number of leading UK architects including Norman Foster, Richard Rogers, Nicholas Grimshaw and Michael Hopkins began to investigate the potential of manufactured components to make housing, as part of a movement that was to become known as 'Hi-Tech'.

While the one-off homes that were constructed are all well known, at least to architects and designers, none of these efforts were to lead to large-scale production. Nonetheless, these projects continue to influence those architects with a particular interest in production as a design discipline and a way to make better housing and perhaps the architect does have a greater role to play in defining an approach to manufacture after all?

Rather than accepting the constraints of systems emerging into the marketplace, architects should collaborate more closely with manufacturers to help define the regulatory requirements and customer expectations to develop the very best system to meet the needs of the housing market. This approach requires a more in-depth knowledge of the manufacturing process on the part of the architect, expanding the knowledge and expertise of the profession and transforming reputations.

Dyson Village
Malmesbury, Wiltshire

FACTS

Location	Malmesbury, Wiltshire, SN16 0RP
Planning authority	Wiltshire Council
Client	Dyson Institute of Engineering and Technology
Contractor	Beard (for the Roundhouse), Carbon Dynamic (for the pods)
Modular manufacturer	Carbon Dynamic
Module construction	Cross-laminated timber (CLT)
Architect	WilkinsonEyre
Start date	January 2018
Completion date	May 2019
Construction period	28 months
Number of homes	67 student rooms
Number of modules	67
Storeys	3

The relationship between architect WilkinsonEyre and the Dyson company has built up over 20 years of working together in the true spirit of working in partnership to find continuous improvement – reflecting the famous Dyson philosophy of design innovation through trialling and prototyping. Having previously masterplanned the Malmesbury Campus in rural Wiltshire for the Dyson Institute of Engineering and Technology, WilkinsonEyre designed this student housing for first year undergraduates arriving at the Institute. The student village provides 67 rooms, each formed of a single 26sqm module measuring 8x4x3m manufactured in cross-laminated timber (CLT). The modules are wrapped in insulation, to further improve the performance of the already significant insulating properties of the timber, and clad in aluminium, while internally the CLT is left exposed. In plan the modules are paired, with some slid apart and in sections stacked up to three high. In some cases the third level modules have been rotated perpendicular to those below, creating a daring cantilever presumably in part to demonstrate the full structural capabilities of the CLT modules, and also to provide moments of shelter and encourage interaction between residents. The stacks are then arrayed in a quarter circle orientated to a communal dining hall to the north-west. The end of each module is fully glazed and set deep into the module to minimise overheating and provide a degree of privacy, and sliding doors within the end screen provide natural ventilation and help connect the residents to the rolling Wiltshire landscape beyond. The irregular juxtaposition of the modules in both plan and section is enabled by each module being fully self-sufficient without any internal connecting spaces. This increases the extent of external wall and so it is assumed that cost was not a primary driver here, but the arrangement does create a memory of Moshe Safdie's seminal Habitat 67. With modules fully factory finished with bathrooms and built-in furniture, mostly in CLT, the warm interiors contrast with the sharp engineered exterior.

Fig 7
The designed pods are arranged in clusters and made from sustainably sourced CLT.

Student housing for Dyson Institute, WilkinsonEyre, Malmesbury Campus Wiltshire, 2019

THE COMPLEXITY OF HOUSING DESIGN

Designing modern housing is a complex task. Architects aim to create homes that inspire and uplift, in a safe and secure environment that supports the health and well-being of its residents. There are often challenges at planning, to respond to the local context and satisfy local residents and the occasional whim of planning committees. Meanwhile housing design requires compliance with a multitude of regulations that set constraints on the designer who needs a detailed knowledge of them all to design compliant homes that can be built. Standards vary according to geography, with guidance such as the London Housing Design Guide demanding different requirements to the counties immediately surrounding the city. The Nationally Described Space Standards remain an optional requirement set in planning according to the policy of each local council across the UK. Many developers and housing associations have a further set of their own standards, often only partially compatible with local planning requirements, and then there may be additional requirements dealing with accessibility, sustainability and housing quality with potentially conflicting requirements.

When the requirements of building regulations, the limitations of materials – building technology and the logistics of production and transportation are overlaid on these standards, the task for the housing manufacturer becomes rather mindboggling. In this the role of the designer increases in importance in helping to balance all of these requirements to determine the most appropriate means of compliance while producing a well-considered design. Architects are well placed to configure solutions that meet the standards, assist with the manufacturing process and above all ensure that great housing is built, to form popular places to live.

Some modern housing is standardised, some of it is well designed, but much of it is demonstrably poorly designed, demonstrating that regulation and standards do not in themselves lead to good design. Much of the housing production worldwide does not involve architects at all. The challenge for the architect in designing manufactured housing is to understand thoroughly the constraints that manufacturing imposes on the design process, and how the design is affected by the manufacturing process. A thorough knowledge of this will enable the designer to be in control of the concept and detail of building design and to be in a position to lead the process.

THE NEED FOR TEAMWORK

All the major innovations in manufactured products in recent years have come from teams which included specialists in design, engineering, marketing, customer relevance, material sciences and other disciplines working together to enable a highly manufactured product to come to the market successfully. The romantic notion of the lonely genius toiling away in the garage for years to produce something disruptive and baffling to the incumbents, but beguiling to the market, should have died many years ago. Unfortunately it lives on in the minds of many, including some of those working in the built environment. As manufacturing has become more sophisticated, the need for design teams to be composed of groups of specialists is necessary for success, as the task of designing high-quality buildings has become too complex for a single mind to encompass all the knowledge required.

This is in stark contrast to the lack of effective teamwork that characterises the design and construction of much of the housing in the UK. Design, production and construction knowledge is kept in separate silos, avoiding the opportunity to combine knowledge to find better outcomes. Standardisation is used to establish compliance and drive down costs without consideration of value as the tender process encourages a race to the bottom.

By contrast, a manufacturing-led approach looks at the available materials and tries to use them as cost-effectively as possible to produce a high-quality result. This minimises work in the process, for example by using sheets of plasterboard at their full size instead of wasting material by cutting them down, or by using one size of steel channels instead of several. This enables the team to produce cost-effective designs which may provide increased space, and improved performance and be delivered more quickly than traditional construction, but at a similar cost. By connecting the many parts of the industry together a manufacturing-led method (design for manufacture and assembly – DfMA) makes that first design a very knowledgeable one which is capable of being realised in a practical and efficient way, but which also embodies knowledge of what makes high-quality housing.

A KNOWLEDGE-SHARING ECONOMY

The knowledge gleaned from working on multiple manufactured buildings spans many aspects of manufacturing and business. Manufacturing businesses differ in key ways from traditional contractors; for example, a factory needs a continuous throughput of materials to operate effectively and prefers a long-term relationship with clients to one which stops and starts around individual projects. The set-up costs of a typical housing factory can vary enormously, depending on the system to be used, but once in operation it has a substantial overhead which needs a pipeline of work to be successful. Like any business, a factory needs to know where its workload is coming from in order to maintain its staffing levels, to train its people and to invest in research and development.

Part of the challenge that architects working with manufacturing face is that, in order for manufacturers to thrive, they need to be fed with an appropriate pipeline of work that is designed to be suitable for manufacturing, and architects are in a position to do this. By designing more and more schemes which are ready for manufacture, or DfMA, the design professions can enable these businesses to grow and thrive, because they will be able to see work ahead and invest in it. Over time this will enable them to bring down their costs and to compete successfully with traditional contracting.

DESIGNING FOR MANUFACTURERS

Manufacturers of fabricated homes often develop detailed product types or house types in a pattern-book and offer these to clients as evidence of their expertise and experience. They do this in order to be convincing to the market on the one hand and to be confident about their cost of manufacture on the other. When they offer a predesigned house or apartment to a client, they understand the cost of production down to the last nut and bolt for the parts of the home that they produce. Knowing this level of detail enables them to reliably predict

Fig 8
Mill Way, HTA Design LLP, Cambridgeshire, 2018

Fig 9
Floor plans of an Innerspace 3 bed house type.

Mill Way, HTA Design LLP, Cambridgeshire, 2018

Fig 10
ilke Homes module installation.

Chase Farm, Keepmoat Homes, Nottinghamshire, 2018

the cost of the home and the timescale for manufacturing it, when they will have production space in their factory.

For many clients this presents an ideal scenario. They can order a predesigned home that fits their needs (assuming that it does), and they can order it from a single source in a relatively straightforward transaction.

However, many of the products designed by manufacturers are not of a high design quality because, being manufacturers, they have allowed the efficiencies of the manufacturing process to drive the design and ignored aesthetic considerations, including whether the result is acceptable to design-conscious planners or neighbours of future developments. When the product in question is a home that needs planning permission to be developed, this throws the problem into sharp relief. Planning authorities in the UK who are often criticised for giving planning permission to housebuilders to carpet green fields with rows of identikit houses may not be keen to repeat the mistake with manufactured homes. There is still a stigma attached to prefabrication in the UK stemming from some past large-scale building failures which still resonate with planning authorities who need convincing that an innovative approach to development with manufactured homes will be high quality and well designed.

Clients such as housing associations and local authorities are bound by procurement rules to use competitive tendering processes to acquire new homes. They are often uncomfortable about this, and even unable to procure new homes from a manufacturer who may not have a track record with them and who may not be very financially robust. They are often required to ensure that there is a minimum number of tenderers competing to deliver a project and if each manufacturer offers a slightly different product, they may feel unable to rule that the competition has been fair.

If a contract is awarded to a single manufacturing entity, they argue, there are risks attached to the delivery. What happens if the factory goes into administration during the project, or if there is a systemic failure with the system? Sensibly, one might think, these are real risks but manageable ones, and are not so different in scale from the risks in traditional contracting.

A realistic comparison between traditional contracting with its many actors and complex contractual trail might easily conclude that a manufacturing approach may concentrate risk in one place but that the risk is therefore easier to manage than the risk of traditional design and build.

A potential route through these risks to a more manufacturing-led industry is one where the designers take a greater level of responsibility for the manufactured product. Instead of the manufacturers owning the system and products, the designers and clients own the system and products and then manufacturers are asked to tender to manufacture a number of products based on the system for a specific project. In this way a group of selected modular manufacturers could be asked to tender a housing scheme based on a reference design with complete manufacturing details and specifications similar to a construction contract with a full specification and bill of materials with no design and build element.

Currently many different manufacturers are operating in the UK with very similar manufacturing processes and systems and this approach would encourage harmonisation and competition among them. It would also limit the amount of research and development they would do, and it would focus their efforts on improving manufacturing processes and not technical competence.

THE MODULAR HOUSING HANDBOOK

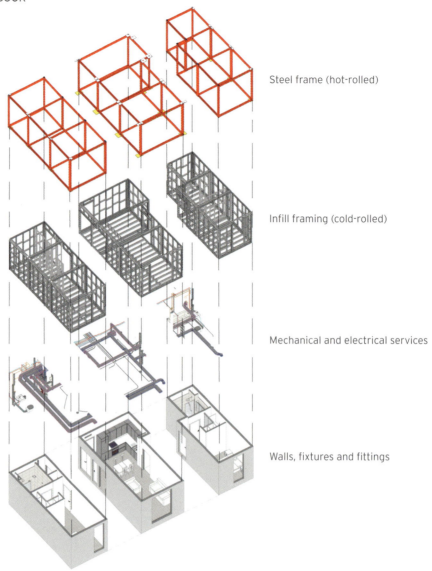

Steel frame (hot-rolled)

Infill framing (cold-rolled)

Mechanical and electrical services

Walls, fixtures and fittings

It is likely that both strategies will be in operation in coming years as the amount and scale of manufacturing grows, where individual manufacturers lead on design and implementation or where consortia of clients work with designers on a more client-led approach.

REPETITION AND CUSTOMISATION

Many modular buildings have a large element of repetition in their design, as is natural in a project designed around housing. There is no inherent contradiction in this, as once an architect has designed successful apartment or housing typologies, they should use them many times. Most successful designers prefer to design something superlative once and use it many times rather than design something average many times. This works well with a manufacturing process which prefers consistency, but which does not have to be relentlessly repetitive. Unlike the Model T, where 'any customer can have a car painted any colour that he wants so long as it is black',[3] modern manufacturing can encompass variety. A good example

Fig 11
An exploded modular apartment demonstrating the combination of structures, spatial arrangement and the servicing by HTA Design LLP

ARCHITECTS AS DESIGNERS IN INDUSTRY

of this is the Swan NU Living factory which offers many customisation options to purchasers of housing types. This approach is similar to that taken by many car manufacturers who offer options to purchasers of new cars. The result of this approach could be that no two homes produced by the factory are identical, even if they are based on a common approach to structure, services and finishes. Customisation offers housing manufacturers the opportunity to tailor the appearance of their designs to align more closely with local context, whether this is in the type of windows used, external materials, roofscape or other design features. It also offers manufacturers the opportunity to manage environmental performance in a site-specific way by allowing homes to respond to orientation with placement of solar panels or shading that are specific to that location and therefore more effective.

At Beechwood West (see case study, pages 174-181) purchasers are offered a wide range of many internal and external customisation options using an online configurator, enabling over one million possible combinations.

Fig 12
Typology diagram of customer design choices, BIM allows for over one million possible combinations.

Beechwood West, Pollard Thomas Edwards, Basildon, 2019

Addiscombe Grove
Croydon

FACTS

Location	28–30 Addiscombe Grove, Croydon, CR0 5BX
Planning authority	London Borough of Croydon
Client	Pocket Living
Contractor	Elements Europe
Modular manufacturer	Elements Europe
Module construction	Steel frame
Architect	Metropolitan Workshop
Start date	May 2018
Completion date	July 2020
Construction period	26 months
Number of homes	112 one-bed homes
	41 two-bed and three-bed homes
Number of modules	323
Storeys	21

30 Addiscombe Grove in Croydon is a Pocket Living project due to finish construction in 2020. It is one of a number of volumetric modular projects procured by Pocket and demonstrates the potential of this approach to deliver multiple projects when there is a strong link between the design and the economic demand. In this case the design is standardised and suited to modular construction and there is a lot of demand for affordable housing in London. The project is being constructed by Elements Europe and contains 153 affordable homes for local people. The 21-storey building is constructed from steel-framed modules manufactured in Telford. As in many other high-rise volumetric buildings the project relies on an *in-situ* reinforced

ARCHITECTS AS DESIGNERS IN INDUSTRY

Fig 13
Model showing the front and side elevations.

Addiscombe Grove, Metropolitan Workshop, London Borough of Croydon, 2018

concrete core for horizontal wind resistance. The majority of the apartments are one-bedroom formed from two modules, and the two-bedroom units are formed from three modules. The corridors are formed using two-dimensional cassettes. There are 12 units per floor which is unusually high but is considered acceptable due to the low numbers of people living in each apartment. The height of the building is restricted to be lower than the neighbouring '50 pence' tower No. 1 Croydon.

SUSTAINABILITY BENEFITS OF OFFSITE CONSTRUCTION

The industry and the architecture profession is increasingly aware of the consequences of climate emergency, with designers becoming more conscious of the impact that their design decisions have on environment at both a local and global scale. It has been said that to avoid gaps in your building, you need to avoid gaps in your procurement. Currently, buildings account for around 50% of global emissions and the industry has a huge responsibility to deliver more efficient and higher performing buildings to both reduce embodied carbon in construction and significantly reduce energy in use.

The widespread benefits of modular construction are becoming ever more proven as more research is done and projects have been evaluated and this should be a consideration for designers and clients. A recent assessment of the embodied CO_2 of steel-framed modular construction indicates that such projects are typically constructed using much less CO_2 than traditional construction.[4] This is material-dependent and not all offsite construction is necessarily greener than traditional buildings. CLT systems will perform better due to the CO_2 locked up in the material. Other evidence demonstrates that offsite projects are often completed in less than half the time compared to traditional construction, with significantly reduced defects both on completion and over time.[5] A typical building may see 65-90% of the building fabricated in the factory, resulting in a reduction of people on site by 60% and reduction of vehicle movements to the site by up to 80%. This results in a quieter, cleaner, less disruptive building site, and causing disruption for a much shorter period of time, to the benefit of local business, the community and council.

In the factory there is approximately 80% less construction waste and up to 97% of that waste is recyclable.[6] Working at ground level instead of on scaffolding, within a temperature controlled environment instead of being exposed to the elements, provides a safer, more attractive and far more productive workplace. This enables a more diverse workforce and increases the appeal to younger workers, with the average age in the factory more than 10 years below that of those on site, with the added benefit that retirement can be much later – a direct solution to those challenges set out in Mark Farmer's 'Modernise or Die' report.[7] Stable employment in a fixed location enables local people to cycle to work and develop a career while balancing work with family and personal goals. Compared to the unpredictable and peripatetic life of the typical construction subcontractor, the benefits are evident to the individuals, and also to society in traffic reduction.

When considered together, the reduction in waste and vehicle movements, reduced use of concrete (particularly in high-rise construction), the higher performance in use and increased potential to recycle the building materials, all result in a considerable reduction in the use of energy and amount of carbon embodied in the building, contributing significantly to the immediate need to reduce carbon emissions while increasing housing production.

BUILDING INFORMATION MODELLING

The rapid development of digital information systems and the capability of advanced software has helped speed up the adoption of prefabrication around the globe. Not too long ago manufacturing for construction required multiple processes transferring information between hard copy drawings, or software programs unable to communicate with each other, creating a laborious and expensive process. While most manufacturing is based on digital processes, not all are yet fully converted to 3D, although all recent and proposed new factories are based on building information modelling (BIM).[8] The impact on their productivity is likely to force existing factories to invest in similar processes to remain competitive as digital processes replace traditional slower ones.[9]

This brings with it several advantages. The process of moving information from design to manufacture is faster, allowing for a longer design period and more rapid transfer to site assembly. The architect and engineers can work on the digital files until a few days before manufacturing begins and there is less opportunity for error, as different disciplines work collaboratively within the same virtual environment. There is also the potential for more sophistication in manufacturing as machines can cope with many different lengths, sizes and shapes of elements, whereas a process involving people making lots of different things would be likely to generate more mistakes.

Related to BIM, there is a family of digital products emerging with links to manufacturing, such as the recently launched PRISM tool developed by Bryden Wood and funded by the GLA. These tools, which are usually rules-based, set out methods for developing designs based on standardised elements or modules. The power of gaming software is being used to power tools which can take standard elements and very quickly visualise how a site or a building could look if it were made from predesigned digital elements. The placement and relationship of these elements to each other can be controlled using algorithms based on regulation or experience. The theory is that some elements of design can be codified into software, and the result can be useful to designers, although in themselves these are not design tools that are likely to result in good architecture. Indeed, one should guard against over-reliance on the software or systems to produce an outcome that fully complies with complex briefs or indeed creates a great place to live. It is more likely that such tools will be powerful aids to designers and enable them to optimise their designs at regular intervals during the design recess, rather than providing a starting point.

Felda House
Wembley, London

FACTS

Location	North End Road, London, HA9 0UU
Planning authority	London Borough of Brent
Client	Tide Construction Ltd
Main contractor and developer	Tide Construction Ltd
Modular manufacturer	Vision Modular Systems
Module construction	Steel frame and concrete slab hybrid
Architect	HTA Design LLP
Start date	May 2013
Completion date	July 2015
Construction period	12 months
Number of homes	450 student rooms
Number of modules	529 modules
Site area	0.16 hectares

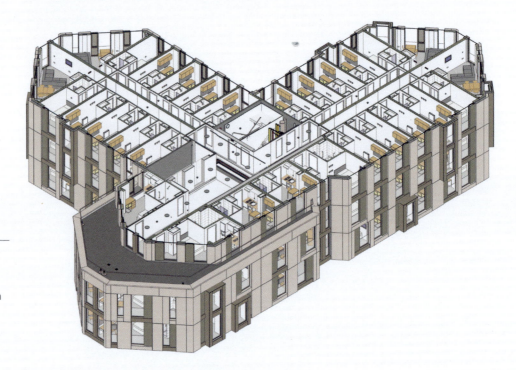

Fig 14
The complex form was developed using BIM Level 2 resulting in zero co-ordination defects.

Felda House, HTA Design LLP, Wembley, 2015

Fig 15
Each of three wings are articulated as a separate element forming slim stepping towers.

Felda House, HTA Design LLP, Wembley, 2015

Felda House is the first of three student projects in Wembley designed by HTA for developer/contractor Tide Construction and their sister company Vision Modular Systems, and followed the completion of Shubette House at 5 Olympic Way, located to the south of this site.

The site had the benefit of an existing consent for an apart hotel but of such a peculiar shape and form it seemed unlikely it would ever be developed. Nonetheless, the consent had established a building envelope that was acceptable in planning into which a new design was developed. Conceived as a cluster of stepped towers based around a T-shaped plan the planning requirements dictated that this would need to be rotated to sit diagonally within the square site, creating a number of chamfered corners. The arrangement of the cluster flats – groups of five or six en suite bedrooms with a shared common room and kitchen, enabled repetition of the basic room type coupled with a rather more complex triangular common room. The recessed upper floors also provided some structural challenges to maintain loadings in line with the deeper modules below. The elevation groups windows over multiple floors including a number of multi-storey oriel windows, which give the building a coherent whole albeit for quite a complicated form.

The building provided a further opportunity to demonstrate the potential speed benefits of modular construction with the whole project completed in under one year.

QUALITY OUTCOMES

Designers in the housing sector always stress that the outcomes of manufacturing processes must be good ones, and they have little interest in fostering the use of manufacturing simply for its own sake. The results must be of appropriate quality to the building that is required and must deliver a sustainable outcome for the project team, the client and, most importantly, the eventual occupants of the building. Investors and insurers care deeply about the quality of the finished product and are already visibly supportive of the manufactured approach. Many mistakes have been made in the past where design quality was sacrificed to the limitations of a construction system and many people's lives were harsher than necessary as a result of poor design and construction decisions.

WHERE DO WE GO FROM HERE?

Architects should position themselves to be the primary designers for clients and manufacturers of housing construction systems and develop a reputation in the manufacturing community for understanding the process of design for manufacturing and assembly (DfMA) and embracing the opportunity to work with manufacturers.

Figs 16, 17
Fab House, TDO Architecture & George Clarke, Manchester, 2018

As the industry expands and develops greater expertise and capability, those designers already engaged in manufacturing are likely to reap further benefits of that knowledge and expertise.

The use of prefabrication has advanced so rapidly over the past decade, that the small number of pioneers that have shown the way deserve to be congratulated, but the sector needs many more manufacturers to mature in the market to provide sufficient capacity and competition. Greater championing of the sector from design professionals focused on designing for factory production would help encourage this much more rapid growth.

Some manufacturers have established in-house design teams, including architects with a sophisticated understanding of their systems, while others prefer to use external design teams that might bring a wider understanding of the market, along with an appreciation of the fundamentals of the system. Working together repeatedly over a number of projects can foster a deeper, mutually beneficial relationship as the architect gains an understanding of the full possibilities of the system and the manufacturer sees the benefit of investing in delivering new design possibilities through new production techniques. Either way, architects are likely to build much closer and more positive relationships with manufacturers, between architects, engineers and production managers, than is usually possible with more site-based contractors and which required quite a change of culture.

This also presents opportunities for architects to act as designers for specific factories and to develop a regular stream of work which would enable them to expand their expertise in manufacturing, as well as going beyond the traditional scope of architects into detailed manufacturing and even into the design of processes.

PERSONAL REWARD AND BUSINESS BENEFITS

Many of the practices responsible for the design of case studies throughout this book are used to working closely with manufacturers. They have learned a great deal about how a manufacturing business operates and have come to respect the benefits of a manufactured approach to delivering better quality outcomes for the projects they design. Architects with the right mindset can use their creative skill to help further increase the advantages of factory production to the benefit of the design.

Practices fully engaged in the culture benefit from repeat commissions and closer collaboration across the whole team, client, constructor and designers, to complete projects as effectively as possible, and secure new projects for the future. Projects complete more quickly, building portfolios for individuals and a body of work for the practice while enjoying a far less challenging culture than is typical across much of the industry. With the accuracy of advanced manufacturing and well managed logistics of site installation the architect benefits from a more efficient site role, and tends to avoid the poor financial performance during the site stages, when fees drain away sorting out coordination and material substitution.

More fundamentally perhaps, architects have a responsibility to design for a safer and greener future, and are able to achieve this through offsite manufacture.

There is much progress still to be made. Architects should continue to contribute to innovation in manufacturing, bringing their own enthusiasm and skill to improve the DfMA process, and thus build better homes, more quickly, to the benefit of their teams and their businesses.

CHAPTER 5
MAKING SURE IT STACKS UP

Mark Farmer and Donna Macfadyen, Cast

The majority of the commentary in this book, and indeed the majority of the case studies in the latter sections, cover full volumetric modular construction. However, to truly understand how an MMC residential project 'stacks up' in terms of cost and programme, it is important to look at the broader view of all MMC forms and put a discussion of cost in the context of overarching manufacturing principles and mindset. Volumetric modular describes Category 1 of a total of seven categories in the definition framework recently outlined by MHCLG's MMC Cross Industry Working Group. Category 2 (2D panellised systems) and Category 5 (non-structural assemblies such as prefabricated bathroom pods and utility cupboards) are also regularly employed in residential schemes. Each category has its own benefits and pitfalls that can make or break a cost plan. What is true, regardless of the system employed, is that a manufacturing mindset has to be adopted from the start to fully realise the cost benefits. This chapter predominantly covers Category 1, offsite processes; however the MMC framework also covers modern techniques to improve productivity and reduce on-site labour, such as augmenting workers with wearable technology or robotics and time-saving techniques such as modular wiring.

When looking at the whole picture in this way, it becomes apparent that this is not a story of quick cost savings. The ethos of a true manufacturing process is one of improved productivity, quality and certainty, and these are the merits to pursue rather than just focusing on the simple cost of construction. As a consequence of improving these areas, however, whole life costs should also go down, and this chapter covers where potential savings can be found when a true manufacturing process is adopted. However, the wider story is both more interesting and more valuable to a client, and to water down the message to simply 'saving money' would be to do your client a disservice and would perpetuate some of the failings of our industry's 'race to the bottom' culture.

'There is an urgent need to rethink how we build homes, delivering better quality, improved safety, carbon reduction and an array of exciting new career opportunities.'

Mark Farmer[1]

Facing page
Two modules being simultaneously craned into place by Tide Construction Ltd.

George Street, HTA Design LLP, London Borough of Croydon, 2020

THE MODULAR HOUSING HANDBOOK

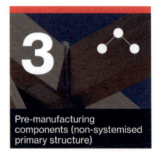

Fig 1
The seven categories from the MMC definition framework that aim to regularise MMC terminology, published in 2019

ARCHITECTS AND COST

There is an understandable fear among design professionals at the perceived reduced role design will hold in an MMC designed scheme. However, the rationalising and systematising of housing design can actually be an opportunity to release architects from constantly reinventing the wheel of efficiency-driven apartment layouts and stacking. Instead, their energy can be redirected towards how the building meets the ground, the facade detail, the urban condition and to understanding the client's needs. The future of MMC is a world where architects have more control, not less. By the same token, a move towards MMC is also an opportunity for architects to take more control of costs. As schemes are designed in a truly BIM environment, assembled from digitally tagged components, accurate live cost and schedule information should be possible. This will shift the control of costs further towards the designers, as a design teams grow less reliant on cost plans calculated at a point in time, and they have a clearer view of how a 'value engineered rate' actually affects the finished product. Clients will cease to rely on the 'mysticism' of cost plans and blended rates and start to assess schemes in a component and product based 'shopping list' online costing world.

This is an exciting development that will help to draw to a close the depressingly familiar tune of a tier one contractor arriving late in the day, declaring that designs are too expensive, and value engineering out crucial parts of the original design intent. A designer helping to refine costs on a job will put savings in the context of how replacement materials will look, feel and sound. They should be thinking of both the architectural and financial implications of reduced floor to ceiling heights, and so on. This design oversight of cost management will all be to the benefit of the client, the quality of the building and the experience of the end user.

COST REDUCTION

The common myth circulating in industry that offsite products save money has to be scrutinised in detail. In net capital construction cost terms, excluding programme savings and portfolio efficiencies, an offsite project is often more expensive. Taking a construction project off site adds administrative complexity that can increase costs, as the construction team is split into factory based and on-site based. Factory set-up comes with its own running costs and haulage of the product from the factory to site adds a layer of logistics to be factored in. Without efficient planning, the cost of embedded factory overheads will not being sufficiently offset by the manufacturing led production savings, unless the remaining site processes with their own overheads are optimised.

In some cases, a modular design will inherently result in higher material costs. For example, the quantity of steel that goes into constructing a light gauge steel frame volumetric module product is often higher than if the same building had been constructed with a traditional site erected steel frame. Most module designs have to self-support during transit and have to withstand the additional forces applied when it is lifted onto the back of a truck and craned into position on site. Up to an extra 25% of material needs to be added to the module itself to account for the dynamic forces present when a module is craned into position, and the steel structure must be over-engineered to absorb this.[2] Internal walls that could have been simple studwork in a traditional steel construction are instead reinforced laterally to prevent the module from warping in transport. None of this should put off an architect but should act as a warning that offsite construction can be a costly mistake if you have not looked at all aspects of the design and commercial sensitivity.

SAVINGS THROUGH ASSEMBLY LINE PRODUCTION

Real unit cost benefits of MMC are achieved when a product is mass produced in a truly 'assembly line' manner. The ethos of bringing the project to the worker rather than moving workers around brings efficiencies in residential construction, as it did for Ford Motors on their early assembly lines. Across the UK market can be found a range of levels of adoption of true manufacturing assembly. At its lowest level, merely engaging traditional tradespeople to complete tasks under a single roof will improve efficiency marginally. More impressive set ups are adopting true advanced manufacturing with moving floors and clearly demarcated linear production processes, saving more time, material and energy, and consequently generating greater efficiencies.

SAVINGS THROUGH MICRO GAINS IN MASS PRODUCTION

A correctly monitored, controlled and repeatable process can be optimised to maximum efficiency – much like the micro gains achieved by a cycling team through obsessive analysis of an athlete's technique powering round endless laps of the velodrome. Completing the same task over and over with a consistent workforce will expose small design and process changes as familiarity with the product increases. Permanently employed staff can retain learning and employ improvements more reliably than a more transient subcontractor workforce. A manufacturer will be incentivised to implement small changes like these as they have better oversight of the accumulative effect than an on-site contractor, where there are far more variables. Material wastage in a factory-controlled environment can be significantly less than on a traditional build. Repetitive construction of closed timber panels (Cat 2) for instance will reduce over ordering, timbers will be cut into lengths more efficiently, and excess material on one job can be used on the next one. All these micro efficiencies will build up into noticeable savings.

SAVINGS THROUGH PROCUREMENT EFFICIENCY

There are also savings to be made through restructuring a project's contractual arrangements. Under a traditional contracting model, a main contractor sits over the top of the construction team and will tender each package of works to a subcontractor. For example, a construction job taking place on the outskirts of Manchester costs £200/sqft to build. A main contractor then adds on the cost of administering the project, site staff and other 'prelims' that are not included in the rates, say 12%. Overhead and profit will then be applied, another 5%. A contractor will then price in the construction risk, a final 3%. A construction cost of £200/sqft has now inflated to £240/sqft. Each extra tier takes a profit, has overheads, and will price in risk to the job in this manner. Under an MMC model, these percentages should in theory be smaller. In a controlled factory setting the risk price should be less to reflect greater control over the product. Reduced on-site works, a reduction in staff and reduction in administration should reduce the prelims, and economies of scale should reduce the overheads and profit. So, although the net construction cost may be higher, say £205/sqft, the percentages added on top are reduced and the overall cost is closer to £225/sqft.

Fig 2
Savings through procurement efficiency: approximate numbers for example only. A diagram showing comparative makeup of total price per square foot for a traditional project and an MMC project respectively

Traditional Project

+ Overhead & Profit	£10	+ Risk	£6
+ Preliminaries	£24		
Net Construction Cost:			£200
Total Price per Square Foot			**£240**

MMC Project

+ Overhead & Profit	£4	+ Risk	£2
+ Preliminaries	£14		
Net Construction Cost:			£205
Total Price per Square Foot			**£225**

SAVINGS THROUGH SUPPLY CHAIN EFFICIENCY

The pattern of savings described above can be magnified if the manufacturer is running a truly integrated operation. In the example above the cost of construction is £200/sqft. This work is passed down to three subcontractors completing packages for £60/sqft, £120/sqft and £20/sqft respectively. Each of these smaller package costs include overhead and profit and risk priced in, and so on down the chain. In a complex job this cascade of profit margins can add up very quickly as the number of tiers between the material suppliers and the client increases. Depending on the organisational structure of the manufacturer these margins may or may not be present in an MMC project. A mature manufacturer that is vertically integrated, with a controlled supply chain and fully employed tradespeople, will hold a larger proportion of the construction contract and thus lower the overall cost of risk and profit margins. An inexperienced outfit building offsite products traditionally through a host of subcontractors will not realise these supply chain savings, and neither will they gain anything from central oversight or long-term R&D on product development.

MAKING SURE IT STACKS UP

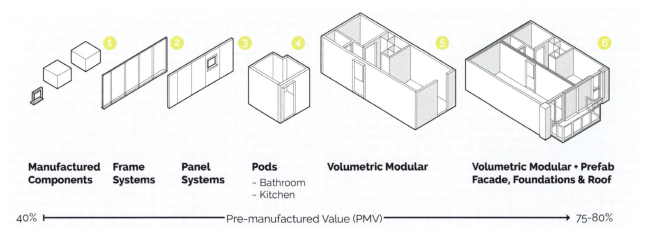

Fig 3
How system choice affects PMV

Savings increase as the percentage of pre-manufactured value (PMV) of the product increases. The savings achieved by bathrooms or utility stacks (Cat 5) should increase in a similar way to whole building modules mentioned above (Cat 1). At the higher levels of achievable PMV (the usual achievable range for residential schemes is between 40 and 80%) such a large proportion of the works is held by the manufacturer that the benefits of working under a main contractor start to diminish. A main contractor would apply a full mark-up to the single high value of the offsite package, despite little coordination being necessary. They are also likely to retain the time-saving benefits described above as 'float' in their programme due to their relative inexperience with MMC's efficiency.

As the market matures manufacturers are becoming less willing to sit under a contractor in this way, and as clients gain experience, they are becoming more confident to deal with manufacturers directly. There is a growing trend from full volumetric modular suppliers to move to offering a full turnkey solution, where the manufacturer takes ownership for both the above and below groundworks.

Pre-manufactured value

The innovative consultancy Cast, led by Mark Farmer, have developed a methodology for describing the proportion of prefabrication in a project, called pre-manufactured value (PMV). This is a calculation of the proportion of the project value delivered to site as prefabricated elements. The definition is based on total construction price – (preliminaries, profit and risk, cost of site labour and supervision) and expressed as a percentage of the total cost of the project. The interesting conclusion of their work so far is that the proportion of PMV in a typical construction project is 40–50%, because much of modern construction is delivered to site in manufactured components, elements and systems. By increasing the work in the factory the PMV score of the project increases. The research to date suggests that adding systems like structural insulated panels (SIPs) or cross-laminated timber (CLT) increases the score to approximately 55%, adding bathroom pods can increase it by a further 5%, and using full volumetric modules containing bathrooms and kitchens brings the score to 70% or more.[3] To bring the score higher than this requires the addition of the external facade to the module and increasing the prefabrication of the foundations and services. For low-rise housing the proportion can be greater as some manufacturers are supplying the house facade already attached to the module.

Y:Cube
Mitcham, London

FACTS

Location	36 Woodstock Way, London, CR4 1BA
Planning authority	London Borough of Merton
Client	YMCA London South West
Contractor	SIG Build Systems
Modular manufacturer	SIG Build Systems
Module construction	Cross-laminated timber
Architect	Rogers Stirk Harbour + Partners (RSHP)
Start date	June 2013
Completion date	July 2015
Construction period	6 months
Number of homes	36
Number of modules	37
Storeys	3

Y:Cube is an innovative single-person accommodation design for London Borough of Merton by RSHP. The concept aims to reduce council expenditure on short-term accommodation by providing purpose-built projects to house people in emergency need for short periods. Constructed from timber-framed modules and erected quickly the aim was to house young people temporarily while they found their way onto the housing ladder in London. The units are small, 26sqm each, designed to be very energy efficient to keep bills low, and to be demounted and moved when the temporary need is no longer required. Although demountable, the modules have a 60-year design life to ensure robustness. The units are stacked no more than three high to remove the need for lifts and the expensive maintenance they require. Other projects have been constructed using this approach and more are in the design and planning process.

Fig 4
Each unit is constructed from high quality eco efficient materials, primarily renewable timber.

Y:Cube, Rogers Stirk Harbour + Partners, Mitcham, 2015

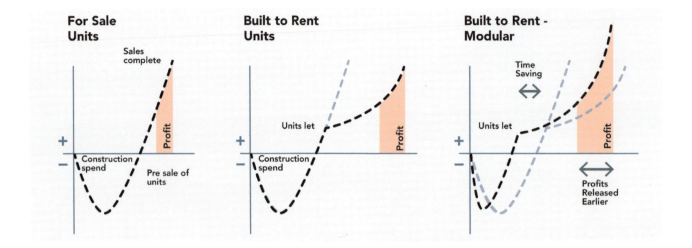

Fig 5
Shorter programme, early release, more profit: diagram comparing the profit profiles of for-sale units and build-to-rent units, and then showing the benefits possible with shorter construction programmes

SAVINGS THROUGH PROGRAMME REDUCTION

Programme reductions possible in MMC delivery can also deliver financial savings of reduced site running capital costs, and through generating earlier revenue as the building is up and being occupied faster. However, earlier completion is not always a benefit to every residential asset class. 'For sale' products are programmed to release units onto the market timed to align with the rate of sale, maintaining a steady supply that keeps demand high. Reducing the construction programme would not always be beneficial in this case and could lead to an oversupply of unsold stock and value reduction. In asset classes such as Build to Rent, later living or affordable housing however, letting-up rates tend to be higher, and earlier revenue has a clearer benefit. In these cases, programme savings are linked to how quickly a product can launch on the market and start generating rental income which will benefit development of internal rate of return calculations.

It is important to remember that a large part of cost and programme risk priced into a construction budget covers works happening below ground, which are mostly unaffected by MMC. Basements and foundations on MMC projects are still usually completed traditionally and the risk cost associated with this part of the work will be largely unaffected by the construction method chosen above ground. (In some cases, however, an MMC light gauge or timber frame structure might be lighter than other construction methods, reducing loads on the foundations and their associated cost.

SAVINGS THROUGH COST OF DEBT REDUCTION

Programme savings can also reduce the cost of debt borrowed for the duration of the works. Construction projects are financed using equity and debt, and the debt on a residential construction project will carry a high percentage of interest due to the high-risk nature of the loan. The longer a construction project goes on the more interest accumulates at a relatively steep rate. A shorter construction programme will therefore result in a smaller amount of interest building up during construction.

In the case where a building is retained post construction, profits from sale cannot always be used to pay back borrowed sums and thus the debt cannot be repaid straightaway. Programme savings can still be beneficial in this case, as the debt supporting the project can

MAKING SURE IT STACKS UP

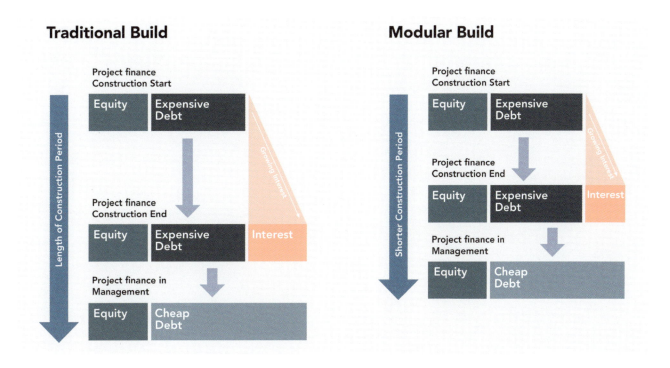

Fig 6
Potential for debt reduction through shorter construction programmes

be restructured once the project is completed. Debt secured against a completed building is considered a less risky position than one still being built and will command a cheaper rate of interest. Therefore, the faster a project graduates into this less risky position the cheaper the borrowing and the less interest accumulates.

Figure 6 shows how a shorter time period for a modular build can result in a smaller accumulation of interest, and a quicker conversion to cheaper debt.

Alongside the cost savings of a shorter, MMC-driven, programme come the risks of the construction debt and payments being tied to a single manufacturer, often for factory products that are not even on site yet. The risk of supplier failure to the client can be extensive. It is much easier to replace a traditional contractor than it is to engage a new manufacturer who potentially has a completely different system. Ways to mitigate this being seen in the market include enshrining in contract that the lender has the right to step in and keep a factory running if an outfit goes bust. Another method of providing some security is young start-ups teaming up with more established outfits who will step in and take on their pipeline should the young business fail. The future of reducing this risk lies in interoperable MMC designs that can be completed by multiple manufacturers.

COST CONSISTENCY

CONSISTENCY OF OVERHEAD COST

The overhead costs in a factory set-up should be more consistent than when compared to overheads of a traditionally built job. Workers on a full-time contract will be paid an annual salary, and like contracting situations in other industries, structured salaries are likely to be lower and more consistent than models where tradespeople are self-employed, repricing their services every time they are instructed on a new job, and are often paid per m² of works complete rather than for a year of service. Equally, a factory with a consistent throughput will require a consistent materials order, reassuring their suppliers and securing competitive rates.

Health and safety issues are a risk on a construction job, and therefore have a cost attached to them whether they happen or not. Although the improved safety found in a factory set-up may not feel like it belongs in a discussion about cost, it all adds to the bigger picture. Work taking place under a roof in the dry and at ground level is inherently safer than if conducted in the varying conditions found on different sites. Work at prescribed stations is easier to monitor for dangerous practices, and hazards in the workplace are easier to spot if your workplace is always the same factory floor rather than a new site every month. At the more sophisticated end of the scale, a workforce kitted out with wearable technology such as VR/AR goggles and exoskeletons (Cat 7) to assist them physically should increase output and reduce one-off accident costs.

CONSISTENCY OF QUALITY

The monitoring of production described above also leads to improved quality of workmanship. Quality improvement is a goal in itself, but it also feeds into a discussion of cost as higher quality reduces the cost of rectifying substandard work, or redoing work that is wrong. A proper assembly line set-up will also have a clearer and more regular system of quality assurance checks. Factories that are more established and are employing precision manufacturing techniques, such as CNC machinery or robotic welding, will also improve the accuracy and consistency of the work. Such work is being produced more accurately, workmanship is being monitored more closely, and products are checked systematically. Once a scheme is up and running, clients who retain the building will benefit from life cycle savings found, as a higher quality and durability should reduce the frequency of elements being replaced and other maintenance costs. A higher quality build should also perform above average on metrics such as thermal performance, reducing the cost of energy bills.

citizenM
Tower of London, London

FACTS

Location	Trinity Square, London, EC3N 4DJ
Planning authority	London Borough of Tower Hamlets
Client	citizenM
Contractor	Balfour Beatty
Modular manufacturer	Polcom
Module construction	Steel-framed with steel floors
Architect	Sheppard Robson
Completion date	July 2016
Number of homes	370 hotel bedrooms
Number of modules	370
Storeys	8

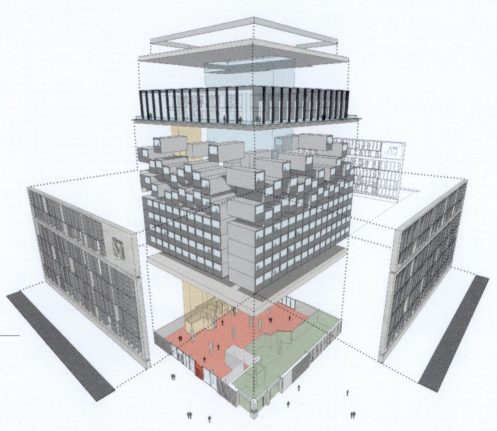

Fig 7
Exploded axonometric.

citizenM, Sheppard Robson, London Borough of Tower Hamlets, 2013

Opened in July 2016, this 370 bedroom hotel demonstrated one of the many benefits of volumetric construction as it was sited over a busy London tube station, Tower Hill, which could not be closed for the works, and the existing foundations had to be reused to minimise disruption and risk. The lightweight nature of modular construction meant that these issues could be resolved by installing the modules overnight when the station was closed and the lightweight nature of the construction meant that a larger building was constructed than previously thought possible. The bedrooms are arranged around a central courtyard and have been constructed using citizenM's stacked modular pod design. This prefabricated method of construction means that the bedrooms benefited from enhanced quality control, which resulted in precise detailing and excellent internal finishes – an essential characteristic of high-quality hotel rooms.

Fig 8
Contemporary architecture that respects the building's historic setting whilst negotiating the inherent technical challenges of the site being located above a London Underground Station.

citizenM, Sheppard Robson, London Borough of Tower Hamlets, 2013

MAKING SURE IT STACKS UP

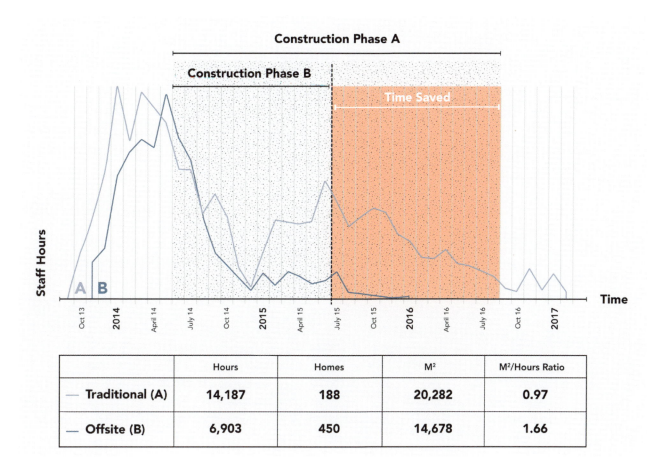

Fig 9
Designers work profile – traditional vs offsite design

A DIFFERENT SPEND PROFILE

Beyond how much it will cost a client, it is also important to think about when they will need funds available and how costs are apportioned across a programme. Funders are often surprised by the differing spend profile on an MMC project, so providing clear guidance on this is important.

EARLY DESIGN FEES

Early engagement with manufacturers is often discussed as important to an MMC job, however this needs to be further scrutinised to ensure it is beneficial. Securing a relationship with a manufacturer at Stage 2 can save time and rework post planning, but it will add to design fees at this point. Early engagement also carries a risk that if they input too thoroughly into the design at pre-planning, the scheme developed will not be system agnostic. This can cause issues later on if the manufacturer changes or goes bust. To avoid this, before submitting for approvals, the design team can reach out to a few manufacturers for a headline commentary on the schemes for alignment with their systems. This is an opportunity to get manufacturers' input on the cost plan, programme and whether the design is optimised for MMC. It will also test manufacturers' appetite for the scheme, how attractive it is financially, and will give manufacturers an idea of the potential pipeline. Testing early interest in this way should not affect fees but does involve a time investment.

Once a scheme has planning consent, it is important to engage the manufacturer straight away under a pre-construction services agreement (PCSA). The manufacturer needs to be involved early, contributing to the design development prior to the building contract being fixed, in order to realise the programme benefits expected from an MMC job. It is also common for this design phase to take longer than in a traditional job, in order to freeze the design before factory production can begin. If a scheme is a predominantly traditional build but employs some Cat 5 elements, for example bathroom pods, these factory-built components may require additional consultants and coordination effort, affecting design fees. All this extra work will come at a cost, earlier than your client and their funder might expect.

For projects embracing MMC at a larger scale there may be research and development costs early on. These can provide benefits too, since smart clients are able to use the outputs of R&D to evolve their brief and develop their products. Equally, given the 'new' nature of some forms of MMC there may be more fees spent in general design due diligence to provide client comfort, such as going to see several factories, building and testing full prototypes and so on. Depending on the level of experience in both the client and design teams, there may also be an element of upskilling necessary, which all contributes to cost. The recently released GLA PRISM app is an example of a tool designed to augment designers' knowledge of MMC systems while not stifling the creative design process.[4] It is a good example of how the market and government are responding to the need to upskill clients and designers on embracing MMC in the early design phases. By gifting this software to the industry as open source, the barrier to learning about design and construction parameters has been lowered to encourage even the merely mildly curious. As the general level of knowledge rises across the board, additional costs in this area should become lower.

IN CONSTRUCTION

Mobilising a manufacturer is different to mobilising a traditional contractor. An efficient manufacturer will be running a full-time operation at the factory, with permanently employed staff. A steady stream of work is essential for business success, and so manufacturers will be keen to secure a pipeline of work and block out a full diary of production. As a result, booking the factory slot, and paying a fee for this, is important. For the client it is important to lock down production start times that keep the project to an efficient programme; for the manufacturer it is important that the client knows that moving or cancelling the slot comes at a cost.

Once production is up and running an efficient MMC programme should be considerably shorter than a traditional build. This will result in the monthly draw down being compressed into a shorter timeframe. With competent planning it is possible to run the offsite packages in parallel to those on site. Cat 2 SIPs panel construction, for instance, can take place offsite, while foundations are being laid on site. Cat 5 utilities stacks can be assembled concurrently with the RC stair and lift core they will sit inside. Cat 1 rooftop modules can be built to their own programme while the building they will sit on may be built on site from traditional construction.

In securing the design early to try to achieve additional efficiency savings you run the risk of aligning too closely to a single manufacturer's specific system. Designs can be developed to be efficient for MMC while also being agnostic to different manufacturers. Refining the design early should focus on designing repetitive components that can be assembled systematically.

CONCLUSION

The discussion above has covered the predominant themes of cost and spend profile when comparing MMC to traditional builds in the current market. Looking ahead, clients embarking on a residential project need to be mindful of the direction the market is taking. The increasing risk of the absence of skilled labour has been discussed at length on many different platforms. Couple this with a housing crisis that is pushing politicians to increase supply at a higher level of quality and with improved carbon credentials, and it all drives a very high demand for a reducing supply of traditional skill sets and competencies, to impossible levels. Architects should advise their clients to be mindful that there is just not sufficient capacity in the market for everything to be built traditionally in what is a tightening regulatory market. Projecting forward into the future, the above situation is likely to get worse, not better. Any client looking at delivering a long-term quality product needs to be thinking about R&D now, getting into the MMC mindset of standardisation and repetition, and building up their brand standards with a component mindset. As we head into the future it will get harder and harder to complete projects using wholly traditional methods and doing so will become prohibitively expensive and risky.

The antidote to the risks described above is the knowledge that, after a very slow start, the construction industry's technology evolution is finally gaining momentum.

Chapter Highbury II
Islington, London

FACTS

Location	295 Holloway Road, London, N7 8HS
Planning authority	London Borough of Islington
Client	Tide Construction Ltd
Main contractor and developer	Tide Construction Ltd
Modular manufacturer	Vision Modular Systems
Module construction	Steel frame and concrete slab hybrid
Architect	HTA Design LLP
Start date	February 2017
Completion date	August 2018
Construction period	9 months
Number of homes	257 student bedrooms
Number of modules	310
Storeys	13

This project is a powerful demonstration of the potential for modular construction to unlock housing delivery on increasingly constrained urban sites. The building provides 257 student rooms and associated common space and amenities within a 13-storey building on a narrow site with frontage onto the A1, a no-stopping Red Route dual carriageway; at the junction with Hornsey Road to the south, which required constant access to the north London waste processing plant and ambulance depot. To the north sits Holloway Road underground station with the Piccadilly Line running beneath. Originally consented to a design by CZWG Architects the scheme was redesigned to account for recent changes in regulations. Along with some internal reconfigurations an additional floor was added within the constraints of the consented heights due to the more efficient storey heights achieved by the highly engineered modular solution.

Revised planning consent was worked up and approved while construction commenced under the extant consent, with a revised consent approved just in time to ensure the building could be delivered to the new scheme proposals. Module delivery logistics were particularly critical given the site location, with trucks stopping for around 10 minutes to enable off-loading and craning on to the building site to happen. Despite the traditional handset brick facade requiring scaffolding and limiting the speed of delivery, the whole design and construction period took just nine months, completing in August 2018 in time to open for the new academic year.

Given the constrained location and a building footprint that entirely covers the site, the constraints on highway closures and the need to provide constant access across the site to a Piccadilly Line substation, it seems unlikely that the project could have been delivered using traditional construction methods.

Fig 10
The design echos the beautiful Grade I listed Holloway Road London Underground station mimicking its glazed tiles and station arches.

Chapter Highbury II, HTA Design LLP, Islington, 2018

CHAPTER 6
THE MODULAR WORLD

This chapter aims to define the extent of the opportunity for UK practitioners to export their experience to other countries seeking to maximise the benefit from offsite construction, in particular Singapore, Hong Kong, China and Eastern Europe.

As the global interest in modular and prefabricated construction grows, an increase can be seen in interest from international clients and technical bodies who historically have looked to the UK for design and technical expertise, coming to see and learn about the work being done in the field in the UK. We are also seeing other countries sending teams to the UK to learn, who haven't had technical links to British standards or regulations but see the prefabricated work that is being done here now and want to emulate it in their own markets. There is a continually growing level of interest internationally and many countries have developed policies specifically aimed at expanding the market for offsite construction or set targets to deliver growth in prefabrication soon. All of this is good news for the sector, but it also raises difficult questions about the exchange of knowledge and information. Should intellectual property be protected from other countries? Are there dangers in sharing technologies from one country with another country that has a significantly different climate, geography or geology that require a unique structural response (for example, seismic activity). It is important that all participating countries and organisations are responsible in their use and sharing of technical information to guard against high-profile problems at a point when the offsite industry is growing rapidly but vulnerable to the effect of a construction failure.

'I want the UK to become the world leader in modular homes within the next 10 years, with safety, quality and choice at its heart.'[1]

Housing Minister **Esther McVey** visiting the Legal & General factory, January 2020

Facing page
Glen Iris Residential Building,
Stoll Long Architects &
Modscape, Australia, 2018

The McKinsey report 'Modular Construction: From projects to products' published in June 2019 highlights that the market for modular construction in the EU and US could reach $130bn by 2030.[2] This is based on their prediction of an expansion in activity in those and many other markets responding to well-known pressures on construction. The reasons why this expansion of interest in prefabrication in general and volumetric modular in particular is happening across the globe appears to be consistent with the message of the 'Modernise or Die' report written by Mark Farmer.[3] Concerns about an ageing construction workforce, a lack of skills in the construction sector, problems created by a migratory workforce, health and safety concerns relating to construction activities, poor quality of traditional construction and pollution from construction activities are all cited as reasons why different countries around the world see prefabrication as becoming an increasingly important part of their construction activity in the years ahead. Because of the work already done here in the UK over the last two decades, British firms are at the leading edge of this type of construction and this is bringing new opportunities and challenges for UK specialists in prefabrication who are interested in operating overseas.

Examples of specialisms that are in demand overseas fall into three main categories: design expertise in the development of typologies suitable for prefabrication (and relevant to the local market), engineering specialists who understand the use of prefabricated systems and structures typically applied in offsite construction, and site-based assembly specialists and process engineers with experience in setting up and managing industrial production facilities which can deliver prefabricated systems or modules. In the last few years there has been an increasing demand for architects and structural engineers who have experience in designing these kinds of buildings as clients who are embarking on prefabricated projects don't want to risk their project success by employing an inexperienced design team. There is also recognition that setting up prefabrication factories is a large investment, and the investors naturally want to protect their investment by getting advice from those who have the most recent and relevant experience in setting up factories, understand the machinery available for prefabrication and understand the role of automation and robotics.

Architects keen to participate in international work on modular projects will need to ensure that they have a solid grasp of the technical basis for designing volumetric buildings and have a coherent DfMA approach and skilled staff to carry out the work. It goes without saying that each market has its own characteristics, and practices looking to work overseas should be prepared for a lengthy period of marketing and market engagement before being able to enter the market. It is always wise to partner with local firms who may benefit from a connection to a UK company with more specific expertise and jointly win work that they would not have been qualified for separately.

The following summary of the activity in some of the larger overseas markets demonstrates the global interest and the potential opportunities for UK businesses overseas.

AUSTRALIA

There is government support for prefabrication with research grants being given to set up an Advanced Manufacturing Growth Centre in addition to funding already allocated to training in prefabricated housing. The aim is to move the prefabricated buildings sector from 3–5% of the industry to 15% by 2025. The Government of Victoria has set up a modular framework of 13 companies to deliver 1000 affordable homes across the state over a three-year period.

The Hickory Group is an innovative Australian contractor that uses a variety of prefabrication methodologies including partially finished volumetric steel-framed modules and has successfully completed the 42-storey La Trobe Tower in Melbourne.

Companies active in the market: Archiblox, Modscape, Fleetwood, CIMC, Hickory Group.

Notable projects: Glen Iris Residential Homes, Victoria. This is a 23-unit three-storey residential building of one-bedroom apartments constructed using prefabricated modules by Modscape. Port Hedland, Western Australia, a 1202-room workers' village constructed by CIMC China. Port Hedland, Western Australia, a 293-unit residential development by Fleetwood. Pilbara, Western Australia, a 3200-room workers' village constructed by CIMC China.

Fig 1
Glen Iris Residential Building, Stoll Long Architects & Modscape, Australia, 2018

La Trobe Tower
Melbourne

FACTS

Location	327 La Trobe Street, Melbourne VIC 3000, Australia
Planning authority	Melbourne
Client	Long River Investments
Contractor	Hickory Group
Modular manufacturer	Hickory Group
Module construction	Structural frame and service pods
Architect	rothelowman
Start date	June 2015
Completion date	December 2016
Construction period	19 months
Number of homes	206
Storeys	43

The La Trobe Tower by Hickory Group is a unique project that demonstrates a slightly different approach to volumetric construction to most other manufacturers in this publication. The Hickory Group uses a modular volumetric system to install the major structural elements, facade and serviced bathrooms in a single lift. The internal finishes to the rooms and some *in-situ* concrete casting of structure are applied on site. Each module has walls and a floor but no roof, which is the likely reason why internal finishes cannot be applied due to the risk of weather damage during installation. The project achieved completion of the 43-storey building in 19 months, instead of a traditional 26 months, a 30% saving.

CHINA

The Chinese Government has mandated that 30% of new buildings will be offsite by 2026;[4] this is motivated by a desire to reduce pollution and environmental degradation from construction. There is a concern that a very unproductive and labour-intensive industry is causing a lot of damage to natural resources through poor processes. There is also a long-term concern that a shrinking working-age population will not be able to continue to use the very labour-intensive processes that are currently used. Some Chinese companies already offer their prefabricated products for sale overseas and while it may seem counter-intuitive to import goods to Europe from such a long distance, the base cost of Chinese companies is significantly lower than in the UK, and the environmental cost of transport by sea is relatively low. Coupled with the fact that Chinese investors finance a lot of overseas development it is highly likely that China-based manufacturing will grow steadily to supply to their enormous domestic market and some overseas markets.

Turner & Townsend, in their summary of the future of the China construction market predict that by 2020 there will be more than 300 Chinese prefabricated-component factories serving China's construction sector, with the prefabricated buildings market and steel structure market worth around 300bn Chinese Yuan and USD50bn respectively.[5]

Companies active in the market: CIMC, a government-owned company that manufactures living accommodation modules for housing and hotels as well as shipping containers. They can transport their modules anywhere in the world where container ships go, giving them access to many of the world's largest coastal cities. Their module sizes are partially dictated by shipping container sizes as they need to be able to stack them on cargo ships to transport them.

Relevant projects: Hampton by Hilton Hotel, Bristol Airport.

DENMARK

Similarly to other Scandinavian countries, Denmark has welcomed prefabrication for many years as their workforce has moved offsite into factories that can be efficient all year around.

Companies active in the market: Scandi Byg are a modular housing manufacturer using timber frame construction to manufacture modules for buildings up to six storeys in height for the Danish and German markets.

Fig 2
Balders Have, ONV Architects – JaJa architects, Denmark, 2013

Fig 3
Innocel, Leigh & Orange Architects, Hong Kong, 2019

HONG KONG

The Hong Kong Government is a major housing provider and construction costs are among the highest in the world. The ratio of home prices to average earnings is 22:1, compared to the London ration of 9:1 and a UK average of 5:1.[6] In addition, Hong Kong's construction sector is heavily unionised and presents barriers to foreign workers. This has meant that the construction sector is unable to grow to meet demand and construction costs have risen steadily. The availability of land is low and consequently the bulk of new buildings in Hong Kong are high rise, often 60 storeys and above, usually constructed on highly constrained sites operating at multiple levels due to the geographical nature of Hong Kong. The design and construction of tall buildings lends itself to repetition and prefabrication and the Hong Kong Government has embarked on a programme of research and development with the aim of introducing modular prefabrication to the market.

Companies active in the market: CIMC, IMAX Modular Pte Ltd.

Notable projects: Innocel, Hong Kong Science Park, 500 residential units of affordable accommodation. The Wong Chuk Hang student accommodation building for Hong Kong University due to finish in 2021, constructed by Paul Y Construction with IMAX Modular Pte Ltd.

Wong Chuk Hang Student Residence
Hong Kong

FACTS

Location	4 Police School Rd, Wong Chuk Hang, Hong Kong
Planning authority	Hong Kong
Client	Hong Kong University
Contractor	Paul Y Construction
Modular manufacturer	Yahgee Modular House
Module construction	Steel frame and concrete slab hybrid
Architect	AD+RG (with HTA Design LLP)
Start date	2019
Completion date	2023
Construction period	4 years
Number of homes	1224 student rooms
Number of modules	c1500
Storeys	17

While the UK housing market has started to attract investment from overseas, countries with a housing crisis of their own, such as Hong Kong, are also looking to the UK for design expertise and delivery experience. During 2017-18, various fact-finding delegations from the Hong Kong Government and boards of trade journeyed to London to observe modules being delivered to site and to inspect completed buildings. The Hong Kong Government correctly identified that the particular combination of circumstances that were driving modular innovation in the UK market were also present in Hong Kong, namely:

- A chronic housing crisis resulting in extreme overcrowding.
- Disproportionate land values demanding dramatically shorter construction periods.
- Declining skills and headcount in the construction sector.
- Increasing cost of labour and worsening problems of build quality.

The Hong Kong Government decided that modular integrated construction (ubiquitously abbreviated to MiC) should be officially encouraged as a strategic solution to these problems and, being the dominant landowner and controller of regulations, and with the HK Development Bureau in possession of significant sovereign wealth, it has a unique opportunity to make its strategic goals a reality.

The student accommodation project at Wong Chuk Hang for Hong Kong University is a pilot project to advance the high-rise MiC sector. The project comprises a pair of 17-storey towers of student residences above a non-residential podium. It houses 1224 hostel places, associated living accommodation for management staff, common rooms, canteen, support facilities and car-parking space. Since the project is perched on a steep site of native jungle (with complex retaining structures necessitating a groundworks programme of approximately 15 months), this provided a good opportunity to tender the MiC component and resolve the numerous technical and regulatory issues before the first modules would be needed on site.

The project has been led by local architect AD+RG, advised on modular design matters by HTA. In addition to technical design input, HTA provided strategic project management and procurement advice to the client through the selection of a main contractor and their chosen MiC manufacturer. Construction began in late 2019 and is scheduled to complete in 2023.

Fig 4
Prime Living, C+W O'Brien Architects, Dublin, 2019

IRELAND

There is growing demand for housing in Ireland. With jobs and population booming once again the demand for residential property is greatly outstripping current supply. Dublin has seen the average rental price surge to record highs as the number of units being built has been drastically lower than demand. Rental costs are rising at the rate of 5% per annum as supply is not meeting demand.[7] Housing demand, driven by high employment rates, is currently at an all-time high, and a large number of developers, backed by international funds, are now focusing on residential projects to address the shortfall of supply. Developers are focused primarily on the Build to Rent, build-to-sell, student accommodation and co-living sectors. However, Ireland is now close to full employment and a number of construction jobs have been added to the Critical Skills Employment Permit to attract foreign workers. A recent Dublin City Council Study estimates that there is a shortfall of 16,000–18,000 student rooms and this is also leading to interest from modular manufacturers.[8]

To speed up the rate of delivery, a number of modular suppliers have been awarded a place on the Dublin City Council Social Housing Framework where 750m euro-worth of housing is to be built using the modular method. This is aimed at delivering part of their target of 9000 housing units to be delivered between 2018 and 2022. Recent relaxations in Dublin's storey height limitations are offering improved construction efficiencies, which may help to make volumetric projects more viable by compensating for the complexity of brickwork facades and the recently adopted, highly onerous environmental performance targets. Developing 3D volumetric solutions in Ireland requires certification in order to comply with local regulations. In this case, an NSAI Agrément Certificate is required to produce offsite manufactured solutions. A number of companies are currently working through this process with project starts on site during 2020 expected.

Companies active in the market: Prime Living, a student accommodation provider, plans to construct a 817-unit student accommodation building in Sandyford, South Dublin, close to University College Dublin.
Essmodular, formerly Extraspace Solutions, a manufacturer of temporary accommodation units and schools, is expanding to supply housing projects in the UK from Irish factories.

Notable projects: A recent initiative by a number of Dublin City Councils saw a showcase of prefabricated homes that could be used to house homeless families. This included examples by Skyclad, Modular Homes Ireland, Spacebox, Roankabin, Portakabin and MOM Services.

JAPAN

For many decades a large proportion of newly constructed homes in Japan have been delivered from a small number of factories which produce individually customised homes based on standardised platforms. Much of Japanese housing is designed to last a relatively short time so it is common for children to demolish their parents' home and build a new one in its place. The ownership of plots tends to stay in a family and speculative housing is a smaller proportion of the market.

Companies active in the market: Sekisui House, Toyota.

Notable projects: Individual family homes produced in prefabricated sections from factories are widespread.

LATVIA

Like other Nordic countries, Latvia has a tradition of timber construction emanating from the wide availability of local structural timber and a need to carry out construction activities during lengthy and cold winters.

Companies active in the market: Nordic Homes, who construct timber-framed modular homes and Forta PRO, who construct steel-framed modules.

Notable projects: Forta PRO are completing work with Berkeley Homes in London to deliver residential projects in the UK. Nordic Homes constructed 'Hope Street' in Liverpool in 2012-15, a development of 339 student rooms and studios up to nine storeys.

Fig 5
Sekisui House: Large opening with deep eaves

Fig 6
Sekisui House: Open living space seamlessly connected to the outside

The Officers' House
Woolwich, London

FACTS

Location	Woolwich Arsenal, Woolwich, SE18 6FR
Planning authority	Royal Borough of Greenwich
Client	Berkeley Group
Contractor	Forta PRO
Modular manufacturer	Forta PRO
Module construction	Forta PRO
Architect	AHMM
Start date	2016
Completion date	September 2019
Number of homes	19
Number of modules	48
Storeys	6

The Officers' House, Woolwich Arsenal was designed by AHMM as an addition to the existing Officers' House. Forta PRO, a modular manufacturer based in Riga, Latvia was appointed to design, prefabricate, transport and assemble the 48 modules on site and carry out final internal finishing of the 19 apartments. Some complex modules were assembled vertically to make duplex units with invisible connections, so some modules were painted after installation. The project is designed to complement the historical value of the neighbouring building but provides modern homes to meet the client's requirements and the occupier's lifestyles, with generous living spaces, terraces and large south-facing openings. The building is finished in hand-laid brickwork to reflect the historical nature of the surroundings.

THE MODULAR WORLD

Fig 7
Brick cladding that compliments the façade of the neighbouring Grade II listed Barracks.

The Officers' House, Allford Hall Monaghan Morris, Woolwich, 2019

NEW ZEALAND

The devastation caused by the earthquake in 2011 has meant that there is far more construction activity needed to repair the damage than the local construction market can deliver. Many UK companies have had interactions with the market but so far, no large-scale projects have been realised. The highest profile project is the 111 Dixon Street apartments project where 228 prefabricated volumetric bathrooms have been imported from a Chinese manufacturer and installed in a 20-storey building in Wellington.

NORWAY

Like other Scandinavian countries, Norway has a long and cold winter that makes construction difficult for an extended period of the year and the construction sector has developed a lot of prefabrication techniques to enable construction to take place indoors during the winter months.

Companies active in the market: EstNor, Astel Modular.

Notable projects: Apartment building complex in Harstad by Astel Modular.

THE NETHERLANDS

In a similar way to many developed economies, the Netherlands' construction industry has moved a lot of production into factories, and a number of companies have expanded from bases at home to serve foreign markets. De Meeuw, a modular steel manufacturer which builds for education and student accommodation markets has worked on projects in the UK and elsewhere. Other manufacturers such as Sustainer Homes focus on the high-value detached home delivered to site with minimal on-site activity. Ursem, another well-established

Fig 8
Leeghwaterstraat, Mecanoo, Netherlands, 2009

modular manufacturer, has worked with internationally renowned architect Mecanoo to design a student accommodation building for Delft Technical University.

Companies active in the market: De Meeuw, Sustainer Homes, Ursem.

POLAND

Currently Poland hosts two companies who export modules to the rest of the EU and to the US. Polcom and DMD Modular are both Poland-based suppliers who have successfully entered the market at home and abroad, shipping their products as far away as Manhattan. Polcom have constructed a number of large-scale buildings in the UK including the citizenM hotel at Tower Hill and DMD Modular are constructing the AC Hotel New York NoMad 26-storey high-rise hotel for Marriott in Manhattan at 842 Sixth Avenue.

Companies active in the market: Polcom, DMD Modular.

Notable projects: AC Hotel New York NoMad.

SINGAPORE

In 2017 the Building and Construction Authority announced a major drive to promote the use of offsite construction. They define volumetric modular construction as prefabricated prefinished volumetric construction (PPVC). Their target is to build one-third of new homes using this methodology and they have begun this drive by requiring its application on government-funded developments. Much of the PPVC work done to date has used precast concrete; it is the only country, so far, to build significant projects using this technology. This method is being used because it is closest to traditional construction methods and they expect it to be readily accepted by the housing market used to heavyweight construction. A recent project, Clement Canopy, was constructed to 40 storeys using this methodology by Dragages Singapore Pte Ltd, a subsidiary of Bouygues, the French construction company. It is notable that the project required the two largest construction cranes in Asia to hoist the 40 tonne modules into place. The modules were constructed in Malaysia, shipped to Singapore and fitted out in a local factory and then installed on the site. A feature of this approach is that high-strength grout is used to fix the modules in place and enables multiple modules to form a single coherent structure. This approach also means that the modules cannot be separated at the end of the building's life and the building must be demolished in a manner similar to a traditional building.

Companies active in the market: Dragages Singapore, a member of the Bouygues Construction Group.

Notable projects: Clements Canopy, a 40-storey apartment building completed in 2018. Woodleigh Lane, six 15-storey apartment buildings with a total of 805 apartments, due for completion in 2020.
Crowne Plaza Hotel, a 243-room hotel constructed using steel modules from Beijing, China.

SWEDEN

In common with other Scandinavian countries, Sweden has embraced prefabrication for many decades as a way of construction which can be continued throughout their difficult winter. This enables homes to be provided in particularly harsh climate conditions without exposing workers to extreme temperatures for lengthy periods.

Companies active in the market: Lindbäcks, a developer, contractor and manufacturer of volumetric modular wooden-framed homes for the Swedish and Finnish markets. They produce 2000 units per year for their clients. Bo Klok, an offshoot of IKEA, the famous flat-pack furniture chain, makes modular affordable homes for sale across Scandinavia. They offer a standardised set of typologies to the market, aimed mainly at the entry level for new homeowners. They have completed 11,000 homes over the last 20 years since starting work in 1997. They are active in Sweden, Norway, Finland and the UK. Trivselhus, a developer and manufacturer of prefabricated sustainable homes, manufactured in Sweden and used in developments in Scandinavia and in the UK.

Notable projects: Titteridamm, Gothenburg, a 152-apartment scheme under construction by Lindbäcks.

UNITED KINGDOM[9]

Pressure on the UK housing market is at an all-time high as several factors, political and economic, have operated to slow down delivery and drive up the costs of housing in the country. There is an annual shortfall of over 100,000 homes which has accumulated considerable pent-up demand and continues to affect costs of new homes and increases demand for rental homes. The affordability ratio sits at around 9:1, a ratio comparing average London wages to average house prices, an all-time high.[10] Government is putting pressure on delivery through its housing body Homes England which is marketing some government-owned land with targets for offsite construction and seeking guarantees of the speed of delivery, but this is too little to make any significant impact. More telling is the investment by Homes England into Urban Splash to speed up their factory development process and the awarding of substantial development sites to them, a signal to the housing industry that disruptive developers are welcome. This has been followed by an investment by Sekisui Homes from Japan into Urban Splash and by Goldman Sachs into TopHat, signs that investors feel that housing manufacturers are good value for money.

While the student accommodation market and hotel market in the UK are mature and volumetric modular is well-established as a delivery approach, it is still relatively rarely used in low-rise housing and homes for rental. A clutch of new projects currently under way or recently constructed is changing that mindset, and many projects are under construction, or in the design stages. Many of the manufacturers listed below are expanding or have had recent investment which will enable them to expand their operations.

THE MODULAR WORLD

Fig 9
Hope Street, FCH Architects and Hester Architects, Liverpool, 2015

Companies active in the market: Vision Modular Systems and their sister company Tide Construction Ltd. Elements Europe, Caledonian, Urban Splash, TopHat, the McAvoy Group, Ideal Modular and others.

Notable projects: 101 George Street, a 44-storey modular development of 536 apartments for private rental, the tallest modular structure in the world at the time of going to press. Apex House, a 28-storey student accommodation building in Wembley, London. Both projects by Vision Modular Systems and Tide Construction Ltd. Hinkley Point C accommodation for workers on a new nuclear power station comprising 44 buildings for 3000 workers, constructed by Caledonian. Union Wharf, a 249-unit apartments for rental development by Essential Living, using modules constructed by Elements Europe. This development consists of a 23-storey and 12-storey apartment buildings near Greenwich, London.

UNITED STATES

North American volumetric modular opportunities are driven by project budgets which are higher on the east and west coasts. Transportation from each coast towards the inner states is hampered by transportation costs. To put this in context, the cost of shipping a fully finished module from Poland to New York is the equivalent to trucking 400 US road miles. Clearly only exceptional economic drivers would justify a variation to this premise resulting in the use of European modules being used for a number of high-profile projects in New York. In some circumstances, river shipping may allow inland options. Volumetric modular manufacturers that serve the inner states tend to use timber modules, normally limited to five storeys, and this is typically used for suburban hotels and apartments.

While all geographical markets have their own certifications and standards, in the US construction market, like Hong Kong and unlike the UK market, design and build procurement is rare and, particularly with significant projects, the Architect of Record (AoR) issues and approves the design, reminiscent of the traditional UK contracts of the late 1980s/1990s. In effect, the issuing, submitting and approval of design and specifications becomes an elemental analysis between the AoR and the supply chain. Realistically, given the nature of volumetric modular products, this piecemeal approval methodology is not suited to the

Fig 10
citizenM New York Bowery Hotel, Concrete Architectural Associates and Stephen B. Jacobs Group, New York, 2018

THE MODULAR WORLD

Fig 11
citizenM New York Bowery Hotel, Concrete Architectural Associates and Stephen B. Jacobs Group, New York, 2018

combined nature of a volumetric product and requires an AoR and their advisors to be experts in the volumetric modular sphere.

To counter this difficulty, companies such as Skystone, a New York-based general contractor holistically ignores the obvious contractual opportunities in this procurement procedure and performs a 'pseudo design and build hand-holding' solution, retrospectively ticking the appropriate boxes, and takes on far more responsibility for the design in order to realise the overall project. Done correctly, the AoR's team emerges from the experience with a far fuller understanding of cutting edge volumetric modular, to inform the next project. It is unlikely that the AoR situation will change soon, therefore the best approach is to ensure that a partnering arrangement is agreed from the outset.

Companies active in the market:
- Forest City, the developer of 461 Dean Street.
- Full Stack, a modular manufacturer that has emerged from the 461 Dean Street project.
- Guerdon Modular Buildings, based in Boise, Idaho. They constructed the 354-room Marriott Hotel at Hawthorne California.
- Katerra, a disruptive start-up with significant venture capital backing that aims to change the way buildings in the US are designed and constructed. Its aim is to bring all construction design and services knowledge together and to optimise the design and delivery of buildings, leading to optimisation and multi-project efficiencies.
- RAD Urban, a modular manufacturer based in Oakland, California. They are a young company aiming to construct high-rise buildings using an innovative four-sided volumetric module that omits the non-structural ceiling of typical modules and the second wall adjoining an adjacent module, thus removing one of the common criticisms of this type of construction. They claim that this will enable them to reduce module weight and costs.

Notable projects: 185 Bowery is a 19-storey 300-room hotel developed by citizenM and constructed using modules manufactured in Poland by Polcom and shipped to Manhattan. Garden Village, Berkeley, an 18-building student apartment development delivered as prefabricated modules by RAD Urban.

461 Dean Street
Brooklyn, New York

FACTS

Location	461 Dean Street, Brooklyn, NY 11217
Client	Forest City Ratner
Contractor	Skanska USA
Modular manufacturer	Skanska USA
Module construction	Steel frame with cementitious floor
Architect	SHoP Architects
Start date	2012
Completion date	2016
Construction period	4 years
Number of homes	363
Number of modules	930
Storeys	32

At the time of completion 461 Dean Street was the tallest modular building in the world at 32 storeys, or 109 metres. 461 Dean Street includes 363 homes for rental in a single tower and is managed by Greystar. It was one of the first buildings to be completed as part of the regeneration of Pacific Park in Brooklyn, New York City.

Designed by SHoP Architects and delivered by Skanska USA, the modules were fabricated and fully fitted out in a factory close to the site and brought to site for installation.

Construction was not without difficulty with installation halting after completion of just 10 floors, to enable a dispute between the contractor/manufacturer and developer to be resolved.

THE MODULAR HOUSING HANDBOOK

Fig 12
The building contains 363 rental apartments with a total of 23 different configurations.

461 Dean Street, SHoP Architects, New York, 2016

SUMMARY

As we go to press with the Covid-19 pandemic having an impact on most areas of life and business across the globe, it feels appropriate to say something about how offsite manufacturing can play a role in helping the industry manage its way through and recover from this crisis. It is worth emphasising that factories are inherently safer, cleaner and more easily managed than traditional building sites, that workers can be given proper protection by the factory during their working period and that workers can be more easily supervised than on traditional sites, and their working practices can be changed to ensure that they are working safely and with suitable distances separating them from others. Many factories in the UK closed briefly during the first few weeks of the pandemic to introduce new working practices and then reopened. The crisis also demonstrates the benefits of having a permanent workforce as they mainly live close to the factory and can travel safely to and from work. In the organisation of the factory floor, traffic flows of people and materials can be structured to be in one direction and reduce the risk of contamination; in reality, most factories work in this way already. Finally, training can be given to employees to introduce new working practices and new safety measures by management staff, and communication on changes can be easily managed. This should ensure that in a health crisis factories can remain open and productive while many traditional sites are closed. While the effect of Covid-19 will hopefully be temporary, the crisis provides a further example of the benefits of moving construction from sites into factories.

This quick tour of the volumetric modular world demonstrates that there are many exciting and varied uses of the technology worldwide. Like other manufacturing processes, there are different demands and markets in different countries. Local economics such as the shortage of land in dense cities like Hong Kong and Singapore are driving demand, as well as construction costs and the availability of labour in London and New York. Looking ahead there is substantial investment coming into manufacturing companies worldwide and the likelihood is that the sector is going to grow substantially. So far, there is no 'Tesla' or similar company aiming to revolutionise the market with an aggressive growth strategy, and this may be because most of the manufacturers in the sector have had some years of growth but also some setbacks and they are wary of expanding too fast too quickly. As the market expands it is likely that we will see new entrants come into the sector from other markets such as the automotive and aerospace manufacturing companies, who see some synergy with mass housing. Whatever the future, it is going to be exciting, and we look forward to participating in it. The warning to the profession is, if you are not part of the solution, you are part of the problem!

CHAPTER 7
BUILDING A MORE MODULAR FUTURE

As we have seen, there is the need and the means to drive the completion of a revolution in housing delivery in the UK and, in turn, offer the combined expertise of a reinvigorated industry to contribute to housing solutions internationally.

Over the past decade new modular housing factories have been established and through completion of a growing number of projects, the manufacturing technology is maturing as we begin to see the full capability of this still young industry. These projects provide clear evidence of what can be achieved when we combine the full capability of UK design and manufacturing experience with more collaborative ways of working, showing that there is an alternative to the unsustainable methods and outdated culture of the traditional housebuilding sector.

The projects showcased throughout this book, including eight in-depth case studies in Part II, provide clear evidence of how manufacturers inherently understand the need for greater design involvement, from inception to completion. Long-term relationships between designers and manufacturers enable learning from each project to be carried into the next in a culture of continuous improvement. The completed projects are proving the sector can deliver demonstrably higher quality, with reduced defects and improved building performance, and with greater choice of layout and specification offered to customers. Many of the projects have been delivered substantially quicker than would be possible using any other form of construction and with significantly less disruption to the existing nearby community due to reduced vehicle movements for a shorter period of time. Those involved in the production and delivery of these buildings benefit from better working conditions in more productive businesses. Some manufacturers report that factory workers are on average 10 years younger than on traditional building sites, suggesting an increased appeal to a new generation working in construction. This is further helped by the vastly improved safety record of modular housing delivery, both within the factory and on site. Perhaps most crucially of all, the reduced wastage and more efficient use of material, labour and transportation enable a significant reduction of embodied carbon in construction while improved airtightness and thermal insulation helps reduce energy in use over the lifetime of the building.

It is perhaps no surprise then, that many of the major clients choosing to invest in a modular future, are those companies providing rental housing that retain a long-term investment in their buildings and neighbourhoods. Being responsible for the management and maintenance as well as ensuring that the homes remain attractive for renting customers, creates a different attitude to the quality of both design and construction. This has led US rental specialist Greystar, which manages over 100,000 homes around the world, to enthusiastically adopt modular construction across its portfolio of London projects.

Facing page
Set to be the next tallest modular building in the world, Tide Construction Ltd & Vision Modular Systems.

College Road, HTA Design LLP, London Borough of Croydon, 2020

Fig 1
A module leaving the Vision Modular Systems factory in Bedford

Fig 2
Artist's sketch by Sandy Morrison

However, the suburban housing market is also showing the increased potential that modular housing can offer to purchasers as well as renters with, amongst others, the always pioneering Urban Splash growing its number of sites across the UK and the range of homes in manufacture.

Both of these companies and indeed many others leading the way in the sector are driven in part by foreign investors, who see the potential of the growing UK industry not just in speeding up delivery, but in driving a more responsible approach to development for both the customers and the whole development team.

There are of course various risks of investing in an industry that despite its recent successes remains relatively small and reliant on private companies. This reflects the inherently conservative nature of the industry and has been the cause of plenty of modular business failures in the past, as manufacturers struggled to maintain a consistent pipeline of work for their factories. The new generation of manufacturers have sought to offset this risk through becoming involved in the development process themselves to help secure certainty of pipeline alongside projects procured through other developers. Indeed many of the most successful companies here have established fully vertically integrated businesses as developer, manufacturer and constructor with in-house design teams or established relationships with architects who fully understand and contribute to the development of the system.

It is notable that much of the increased investment into the UK sector has come from international companies with funding often provided by usually risk averse pension funds, whose experience investing in commercial property potentially drives an assumption in favour of higher quality and quicker delivery from factory production.

A further boost for the modular industry has come from the UK Government choosing to mandate greater use of modular construction on sites promoted through Homes England. Quite appropriately the agency describes itself as the UK Government's 'housing accelerator'[1] as it seeks to speed up housing delivery and help secure the industry, through mandating a minimum of 25% modular housing, within an expectation of even greater adoption of modern methods of construction. There has been an increase in housing ministers visiting modular factories and the recent appointment of Mark Farmer, long-term advocate of modular construction and co-author of our Chapter 5, as the Government's MMC champion.

Notwithstanding this significant progress, modular housing manufacturing remains a modest industry producing perhaps just 2% of new homes currently delivering in the UK each year. The engagement from government and signs of changing attitudes to innovation from some of the larger housebuilders could be an early positive sign of change ahead to overcome the huge problems with construction quality and skills shortage across the industry. Further incentive may come from a planned comprehensive review of building regulations driven by the need for improved safety in housing. And as we begin to understand the implications and impact of the UK leaving the EU, there may well be more drivers for change as we seek to meet the nation's housing need, using fewer workers, with a greater incentive to increase our exportable expertise.

For manufacturers there is a need to harness the current levels of investment to grow production and increase capability. But there is also the opportunity to further invest in the monitoring and evaluation of completed buildings to better understand the benefits in delivery and improved performance in use. This would improve the industry's appreciation of the customer's requirements to drive further improvements for existing factories while sharing the data would help encourage new entrants to the market. This would not be at the risk of losing intellectual property or the benefit of experience already built up through many years of innovation, but could just enable a more secure and mature sector to be established.

For architects with a passion for better design in housing, the opportunities should be abundantly clear. The profession needs to adapt and forge a new relationship between designer and maker, working to bring the entire team towards a more collaborative position to deliver better. In doing so architects might hope to move the role of the designer to a more influential position in improving the quality of mass housing, in a similar way to the designers of celebrated mass-market products including bikes, cars, vacuum cleaners and smartphones. In time we could expect to see yet more innovation emerge as increased automation in manufacture, capable of infinite variation to suit customer needs and design creativity, drives a much needed revolution.

PART II
MODULAR CASE STUDIES

The eight major case studies detailed in this section were selected to demonstrate the design creativity that is starting to characterise the full potential of modern modular housing. Hugely inventive with a technical robustness and performance capability difficult to match in traditional methods of construction, these examples show what can be achieved when architects, developers, constructors and manufacturers choose to work together with a common goal to make better housing.

The case studies include the two tallest completed modular residential projects in the world at 101 George Street in Croydon, South London and Clement Canopy in Singapore, both over 40 storeys tall. Three of the projects – George Street, along with Union Wharf and Greenford Quay – were designed for the exacting requirements of the emerging Build to Rent sector, as it expands rapidly across major UK cities, and in particular London where all three of these projects are located. Along with student housing, represented here by Apex House, these institutionally funded and professionally managed projects demonstrate the beneficial relationship between a long-term investor and a construction methodology focused on quality of design, speed of delivery and cost certainty. The affordable housing available for sale and rent at Mapleton Crescent demonstrates the capacity for factory made housing to unlock really challenging sites with award-winning architecture and, along with many of the case studies throughout this book, demonstrates the increased capability of the sector to deliver tall buildings on constrained urban sites. We expect to see more and more modular tall buildings emerge in dense urban locations as the full range of benefits become more apparent through better understanding of these completed buildings.

At the other end of the scale, low-rise housing projects by Urban Splash Modular and Swan NU Living prove that the benefits in delivering design quality and flexibility are no less significant in more suburban forms of family housing. Indeed there is the opportunity of a far larger market which, over recent decades, has struggled to deliver quality in either design or construction on all but a few notable projects. This opportunity is reflected by recent investment into UK modular housing companies by Homes England, the UK Government's National Housing Agency and international manufacturing specialists such as Sekisui from Japan.

This varied set of building types, delivered by various modular manufacturers using their own different systems, use traditional structural materials of steel, concrete and timber, to demonstrate a breadth of innovation emerging across the UK. Each project has been led by a client convinced of the need to invest in better ways of building, while every project shares the common theme of being designed by architects all committed to working more collaboratively across industry, and with a greater understanding of construction, with the goal of delivering better homes within better places to live.

Facing page
Part II The Journey - Modular Construction Buildings by Nerea Bermejo Olaizola, HTA Design LLP

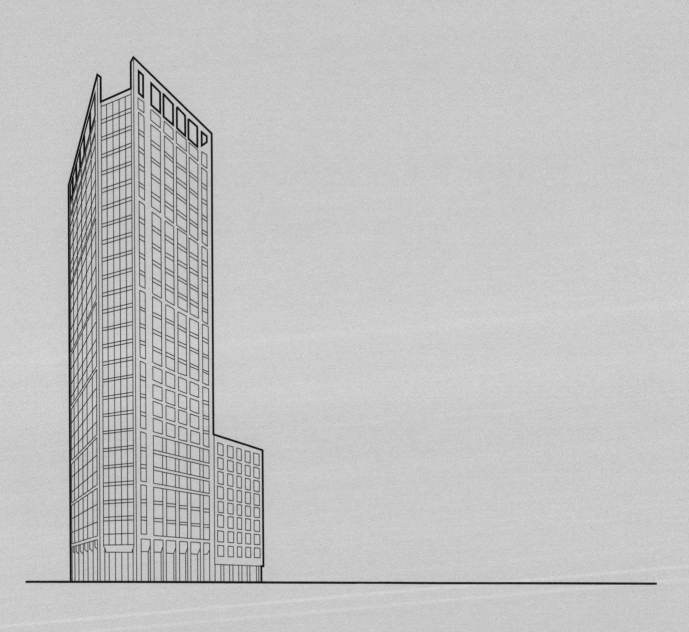

Case Study 1: Apex House, Wembley, London

Apex House was the tallest modular building in Europe when completed in August 2017 at 28 storeys of self-supporting modules above ground, and an additional basement storey, also partially modular totalling 29 storeys of modular construction. Built using the Vision Modular Structures steel-framed volumetric system, the building completes a trio of innovative constructions on the same urban block in Wembley, North London, which includes a 237-room Novotel on Olympic Way, 158 affordable and private housing units on Fulton Road and Felda House a 450-room student accommodation building on Albion Way. Apex House, also known as Scape Wembley, houses 558 student rooms and extensive additional amenities, creating a local landmark signposting the corner of Fulton Road and Albion Way.

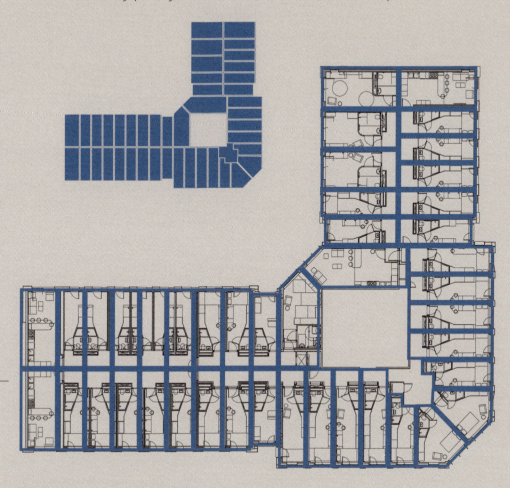

Fig 1 (facing)
Line drawing of Apex House

Fig 2
Floor plan and modular layout

Fig 3
Street level view

Fig 4
An aerial view of Wembley showing Apex House & other HTA offsite buildings in relation to the Stadium

The project was completed within 12 months including the demolition of the existing building on site. This outcome enabled Tide Construction to hand over the project to the operators on time for the student year in September 2017 and to let the building immediately. Compared to a 'normal' construction programme the client gained an additional year of rental income and started to make a return on their investment and reduced their borrowing and financing costs.

Christy Hayes, CEO of Tide Construction Ltd comments: 'Working closely with HTA we have delivered the tallest modular building in Europe at the moment, where design and technology came together to create quality student housing in the capital. Apex House stands tall at 29 storeys, delivered in just 12 months and showcasing the great outcomes we can achieve using modular construction.'[1]

The project team have worked together on a number of developments and use volumetric construction as the default construction methodology. This was the fourth in a series of joint projects involving Tide Construction Ltd, Vision Modular Systems and a group of consultants working together on project after project, recycling knowledge, processes and construction detailing. HTA acted as architects, planning consultants, sustainability consultants and landscape architects. It is notable that this serial collaboration of the same team working together on successive projects is unusual in the UK construction industry and does indicate that the process of manufacturing coupled with strong commercial relationships can work together to mutual advantage.

All four projects are in the Wembley area and all are now completed and occupied. The Vision Modular Systems factory originated in Ireland but moved to the UK in 2009 after the financial crash of 2008 and restarted module production with the Schubette House project adjacent to this building which completed in 2011. The height of Apex House exceeded the structural capabilities of the previous Vision-developed modular system so Vision developed, prototyped and took forward a new structural design for use on Apex and on other even taller developments currently under construction.

Because Tide were the developer and contractor for the site, their brief to HTA was to design a scheme which enabled them to utilise the modular products from their sister company's factory, Vision Modular Systems. This meant that the design stage up to planning consent was carried out in cooperation with the technical team from Vision Modular Systems and the project was designed within the structural principles of their volumetric modules. This meant that there were no doubts about the structural and construction approach to the project and the design team could proceed quickly to final design without waiting for the input of a contractor. The result of that was a building design submitted to planning which was already very well advanced in terms of technical, construction and servicing strategies and was altered very little in the construction phase. This enabled a start on site as soon as planning consent was achieved and in less than a year from the initial concept drawings.

The building is an 'L' shape formed of two flanking wings, one of eight storeys and one of 10 storeys that create a street frontage to Albion Way and Fulton Road and which are designed to relate to the height of the neighbouring buildings. The corner then rises to form a landmark tower of 28 storeys and provides the core to the entire building as well as access to the rear courtyard.

The building creates a variety of room types and shapes suitable for different students including wheelchair units, and a variety of shared social spaces including a café, a landscaped courtyard to the rear and a roof terrace to allow for relaxation, social interaction and group study. There is also a laundry room located in the basement.

As the building is student housing, the team knew that the speed of construction helped to make a business case for prefabrication as it enabled Tide/Vision/HTA to design and construct the building faster than traditional methods would allow. It was designed to be easily constructed using the preferred construction methodology and to attract an investor, as well as enabling the building to win planning and building control approval.

The cellular nature of student housing makes it ideal for volumetric construction as each room is a separate entity and all students are provided with an en-suite bathroom. There are seven different module types in the project to deal with the three different elements of the building, the two wings and the corner tower, and within the tower there are some modules that are triangular to form student common rooms. There are some larger modules for wheelchair adaptable studios and other types that form apartment clusters where students share cooking and eating facilities.

All rooms are delivered to site fully finished to a high quality with all the services routed to a riser located on the corridor side of the modules. This enables the services to be connected to the central systems quickly and easily and avoids any work within the finished rooms. In this project even the bed was installed, as this simplifies the final process of preparing the rooms for occupation and reduces the time taken to install such large items via the lift. It also reduces the likelihood of damage to the corridor and lift finishes from the movement of bulky items.

The modules are made from steel frame and a concrete floor, connected to each other with on-site welded connections and to the slip-formed concrete core with flexible connections for lateral stability. The structural loads are carried down the building through the steel corner posts of each module which align vertically onto the concrete transfer structure which varies in thickness between roughly 1m and 2m and are located variously at ground, 1st, 2nd and 3rd floor levels.

It could be argued that the project was made possible by modular construction as the site was too small to house traditional construction site accommodation and the normal construction activity within the site boundaries, particularly given that there is a

THE MODULAR HOUSING HANDBOOK

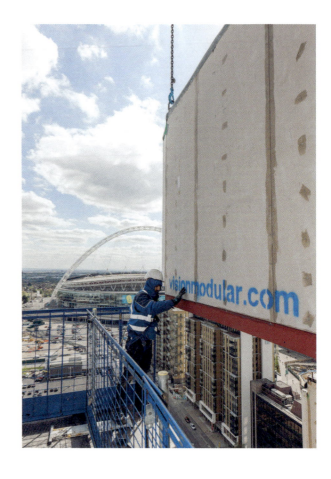

Fig 5
The final module being craned into position

Fig 6
A photographic record of the construction progress

2nd
February
2017

21st
February
2017

2nd
March
2017

6th
April
2017

6th
August
2017

basement covering the majority of the site. The use of offsite prefabrication meant that the building could be constructed by closing one lane of the adjacent side streets for the 12-month construction period. This lane was used for delivery trucks to bring the modules to site and the single construction crane used for the project then lifted them onto the building for installation.

To speed up the construction, prefabrication was also used in the below ground construction in the form of prefabricated reinforced concrete walls and columns. Bathroom pods were manufactured in another factory and added to the modules as they were completed in the VMS factory and elements of the facade were prefabricated to further accelerate the programme.

This approach to the construction resulted in a small workforce, of just 22 on-site staff, removing the need for large areas for welfare facilities and site offices normally associated with a traditional build. It also benefited health and safety – by removing the need for scaffolding and allowing all external work to be carried out from mast climbers.

The facade was applied on site from the mast climbers while modules were being installed, and consists of two palettes of rainscreen cladding system, terracotta tiles and aluminium cladding for the flanking wings while the primary tower is emphasised through the use of polished glass reinforced concrete (GRC) which lends the building a more monolithic appearance. As the crane is in constant use for module installation the facade installation is carried out from mast climbers. An advantage of the GRC is that it is lighter weight than alternatives such as precast concrete, making it possible to use it in this way. Designing the GRC panels required a collaborative process with the facade subcontractor to ensure each panel's size and weight was safe to install while working from the mast climbers. At the same time, the facade expressed the robust qualities for which the GRC had been selected. The detailed design emphasised this by maximising the reveals and wrapping each corner in a singular panel while limiting each panel to a half storey in height. At the ground floor there was greater flexibility as the installation could be directly from the ground and with additional mechanical support so taller storey-high cladding panels were used to create a colonnade which frames the entrance to the building. The ground floor colonnade is mirrored at the roof level to create a crown to the building which sails above the top of the floor to create a greater depth to the facade and frame views to the sky. This crown provided a particular structural challenge as all lateral loading had to be transferred back to the central concrete core not down through the modules and consequently a separate set of steel beams run from the top of the crown back to the core.

The composition of the GRC elevations is organised into a series of grouped floors starting in groups of three and increasing to groups of four and then five storeys as the height increases. This approach was designed to play with the perception of the building and counteract the impact of foreshortening of the tower when viewed from below.

The material palette was chosen to blend in with the neighbouring buildings which predate the project, while the tower is a dramatic white with a polished surface that accentuates its verticality and signals an important relationship with the wider area masterplan still under construction.

A key part of the architectural expression is the chamfered elevation that addresses the street corner and rises above the entrance. To contrast with the brightness and masonry qualities of the GRC cladding HTA designed the chamfer to appear as a continuous surface of darker glazing. This presented a technical challenge as the windows needed to be factory

Fig 7
A view of the building under construction seen from Wembley Stadium

Fig 8
A view of Apex House from Fulton Road

installed while the cladding was done on site. By locating the windows at the front edge of the module and reducing the surrounding cladding depths to a minimum and complementing this with a series of vertical fins the appearance of a unified curtain wall was achieved. Given the southerly aspect of this facade and to further unify the appearance of the chamfer a darker solar control film to the glazing was chosen.

The building has been constructed to meet the BREEAM Standard and includes a communal heating system powered by a gas-fired Combined Heat and Power (CHP) plant. The BREEAM score for the student housing element is 73.2% achieving BREEAM 'Excellent' 2014 Multi-residential. Moving most of the site work into the factory helped cut construction waste to just 2% and, alongside other factors, was key to the project achieving the BREEAM score.

The building was analysed using a dynamic simulation for overheating to reduce the risk of this happening and the window design includes a variety of perforated metal powder-coated screens that shade the opening windows.

CASE STUDY 1: APEX HOUSE, WEMBLEY, LONDON

Fig 9
The modules at an early stage of installation, pre-cladding

Fig 10
A view showing the sympathetic relationship with adjacent developments

Fig 11
Mast climbers putting the finishing touches to the facade

Fig 12
The residents' courtyard to the rear

153

Fig 13
A view of Apex House from Fulton Road

Fig 14
A view of the tower of Apex House from Fulton Road

The tight construction programme meant that the building was fully designed in a short and intense period of activity. The design programme was accelerated to meet the manufacturing programme and to enable the building to be constructed to meet the student term deadline. Everything in the project programme was dictated by that deadline. This meant that decisions needed to be made once as there was little time for changes to be made.

HTA designed the project in Revit from the beginning and coordinated the BIM model with the other disciplines. The modules were designed in cooperation with the eventual owner and operator to ensure that their quality standards are met consistently and that the quality is consistently high throughout the building.

The operators have expressed strong satisfaction with the building, which has been fully occupied since completion.

The architects' experience of working with Tide and Vision has been particularly positive. Because Tide and Vision look for development opportunities and have a volumetric modular factory to construct their buildings working for them will always involve the use of this type of construction. The focus is always on making sure that the building is well designed and capable of being constructed at speed as this gives Tide a substantial market advantage. Many rental investors want to invest in buildings that can be quickly and reliably delivered to meet the needs of the UK market and the use of the modular volumetric system enables Tide to do just that.

CASE STUDY 1: APEX HOUSE, WEMBLEY, LONDON

Fig 15
A view of the main entrance facade

Fig 16
Ground floor communal spaces

FACTS

Location	Apex House, Fulton Road, Wembley, HA9 0TF
Planning authority	London Borough of Brent
Client	Tide Construction Ltd
Main contractor and developer	Tide Construction Ltd
Modular manufacturer	Vision Modular Systems
Module construction	Steel-framed with concrete floor
Architect	HTA Design LLP
Start date	July 2016
Completion date	August 2017
Construction period	12 months
Number of homes	558 student rooms
Number of modules	679
Number of storeys	28
Site area	1876sqm
Operator	Scape

Case Study 2: New Islington, Manchester

Urban Splash were founded 25 years ago and have ever since pioneered a reputation for delivering the unconventional in development. Indeed at a recent celebration of reaching their quarter century, they recalled some of the early advice they had been offered when starting out - "it will never work!" - much of which has proved not prophetic: things seem to have worked out rather well indeed!1

Helping to kick start the regeneration of urban locations particularly in Liverpool and Manchester, but as far apart as Plymouth and North Shields, over this period they have created over 5000 homes.

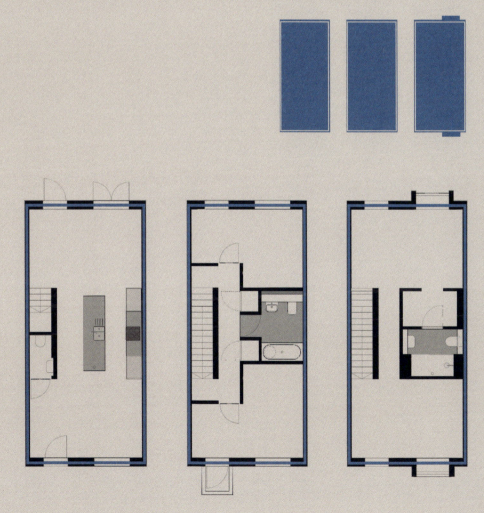

Fig 1 (facing)
Line drawing of New Islington

Fig 2
Floor plan and modular layout

157

Fig 3
Canalside living

Fig 4
The two-storey house types

They built their reputation through the rehabilitation of large urban buildings such as warehouses and factories, often with a rich heritage but having fallen into disuse and disrepair. By converting and restoring buildings into desirable homes they helped entice people back into the city, and helped drive a renaissance in urban living.

This scheme marks a natural transition for the company, as their customers mature and seek to find homes more suited to the needs of a family, but wish to remain living in the city.

A GENERATION IN THE MAKING

The wider regeneration of New Islington in Manchester has been achieved by a 20-year commitment from Urban Splash who took on the challenge of transforming the failing Cardroom Estate into an urban district that is, once again, a popular place to live. Working to an overall vision by the late Will Alsop the regeneration has given numerous architects the opportunity to explore new typologies in housing design and architecture to challenge the norm and help define the place.

Amongst these projects is a truly innovative development of just 43 homes which, though modest in scale, has helped launch a new chapter in the Urban Splash story.

Designed by architects shedkm, long-term Urban Splash collaborators, the scheme has been under development since 2016 and is the first to be delivered under the House brand, creating new build family houses in dense urban environments, harnessing the benefits of factory-based production.

The scheme is formed of three terraces with three-storey homes fronting New Islington and Keepers Quay, which also fronts a short branch of the canal, while a two-storey terrace fronts the new street of Lockyard Lane. Each terrace is divided into groups of five or six homes, for ease of construction and to create access into a private courtyard, enclosed by the three terraces and providing secure parking for residents.

Fig 5
The three-storey house types

Fig 6
Street frontage

Both two- and three-storey house types are based on a standard rectangular floorplate with an area of around 46sqm, which is the same for the upper storeys creating 90sqm or 135sqm respectively for each type. These simple repetitive volumes seek to establish a rhythm and scale quite reminiscent of cherished terraced forms not just from the Georgian and Victorian periods but more recent interpretations such as Span houses. The addition of repeated standard features such as oriel windows and balconies help to enliven the facade and connect the homes to the street as do the generously sized windows.

MOVING TO MODULAR

Urban Splash had plenty of experience of the challenges of delivering construction in dense urban environments and was always seeking to find new ways to improve development. With the homes designed to be highly repetitive externally with internal customer driven flexibility, the decision to pursue a modular solution was a very natural conclusion and led to establishing a relationship with SIG plc to manufacture the homes using cross-laminated timber in their Nottingham factory. It took until 2016 to develop the product from the initial design through a panellised approach to the completion of a fully completed modular prototype, and the launch of the homes to the market. This was facilitated by, and indeed presumably helped drive, the ordered and repetitive approach to the house type design. It also offered the benefit of internal customisation to better meet customer preferences.

This enables customers who pre-order their home prior to manufacture, to choose different internal arrangements, such as the living spaces at ground floor to relate to the street and garden, or on the top floor as an airy loft style, making the most of a vaulted roof space that also helps articulate each individual house from the street.

Kitchens, bathrooms, storage space and servicing have the high level of design consideration and quality finish that is much more easily achieved within a factory environment

Fig 7 (opposite top)
Top floor loft style living spaces

Fig 8 (opposite bottom)
Installing a second floor module

Fig 9 (left)
Irwell Riverside, shedkm, Manchester, 2019

Fig 10 (right)
Port Loop, Glenn Howells Architects, Birmingham, 2018

while the use of CLT as the finish to internal rooms underlines the sustainable qualities of the material.

External homes are delivered fully watertight and prefinished with external cladding part installed, with only minor finishing required on site to connect to adjoining houses.

It is testament to the quality of the design and finish of the homes that having started on site in 2015, all of the homes were bought and occupied by the end of that year. Urban Splash were very engaged with all of the challenges of such an approach including assisting purchasers with acquiring mortgages for such an innovative construction approach. Using this learning to help improve the product and the approach, as a form of R&D not perhaps typical of the traditional housebuilding industry, is typical of the long-term commitment to investing in improved outcomes from one project to the next.

MOVING ON UP

As with all of the pioneers celebrated throughout this book, Urban Splash's move into modular was in part driven by necessity, as they were unwilling to continue dealing with the backward practice of the traditional construction industry, and perhaps a more philosophical sense of what the right thing to do might be for their own business.

The success of New Islington provided the encouragement and momentum to push on into new sites at Smith's Dock in North Shields and Irwell Riverside in Salford, which both quickly sold out and were occupied, further strengthening the benefits of the modular approach.

During 2018 Urban Splash completed the purchase of the SIG factory to create Urban Splash Modular and establish a fully integrated supply chain of developer/manufacturer and ensure effective coordination through complete control of the homes creation process.

This has increased capacity to deliver several hundred homes each year, and the certainty of delivery has led to new schemes at Port Loop in Birmingham and progress on sites at Campbell Park in Milton Keynes with Places for People, and at Wirral Waters in a joint venture with Peel Holdings. This increased certainty has also helped establish Urban Splash as a public sector partner enabling them to secure sites through the Homes England

CASE STUDY 2: NEW ISLINGTON, MANCHESTER

land disposal programme which mandates minimum requirements for the delivery of homes through modular construction.

Most recently this has led to a major deal with Sekisui House, one of Japan's largest home providers with decades of experience in the offsite manufacture of houses and multi-storey blocks and with the expertise to advise on true vertical integration of a developing, constructing and manufacturing business.

Returning to where the journey began with their next project, Urban Splash will be delivering more town house terraces at New Islington. They also will be pioneering the Mansion House concept, also designed by shedkm, based on small groups of large apartments aiming to create a stronger sense of ownership and deliver new-build apartments reminiscent of the loft conversions that first put Urban Splash at the forefront of urban development innovation.

FACTS

Location	New Islington, Manchester, M4 6HF
Planning authority	Manchester City Council
Client	Urban Splash
Main contractor	Urban Splash
Modular manufacturer	HOUSE by Urban Splash
Modular construction	Cross-laminated timber
Architect	shedkm
Type of housing	Urban low rise, customisable homes
Start date	2015
Completion date	2016
Construction period	12 months
Number of homes	43 homes
Number of modules	102 modules
Number of storeys	2 and 3
Operator	N/A

Fig 11
Mansion House, shedkm,
Manchester, 2019

Fig 12
Exposed CLT interior.

Mansion House, shedkm,
Manchester, 2019

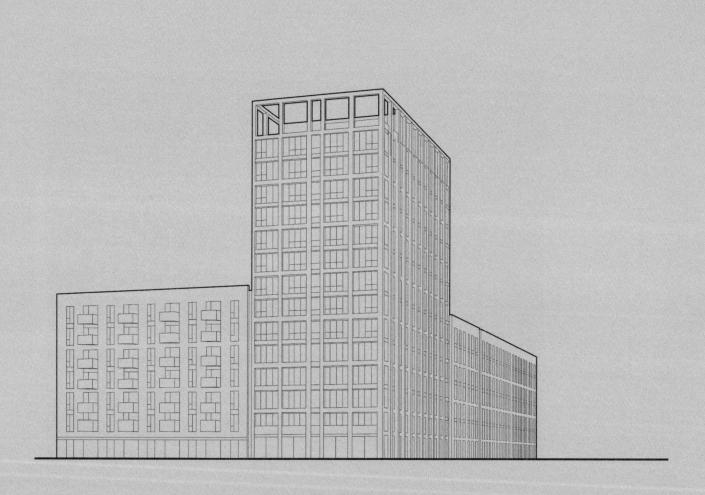

Case Study 3:
Greenford Quay, Ealing, London

Greenford Quay in West London is the first major UK project by US build-to-rent developer Greystar with a masterplan designed specifically to create a purpose built 'multi-family' neighbourhood.

Greystar acquired the site, previously home to GlaxoSmithKline, with a consent for redevelopment with around 600 homes. A revised masterplan was prepared by a stellar team of architects led by HTA Design and including Hawkins\Brown, Mae and SLCE Architects, for over 2100 homes with an increased mix of uses, opening up the canal to the wider area. This was submitted as a single detailed planning application thought to be the largest of its kind

Fig 1 (facing)
Drawing of Greenford Quay

Fig 2
Floor plan and modular layout

165

Fig 3
The completed Tillermans building seen from the Grand Union Canal

at the time, and approved by Ealing Council. The masterplan was based around several new links through the site to improve connections for existing residents to Greenford Station, while a new bridge and a public square was planned to bring the canal back to life.

The first phase, including 379 Build to Rent apartments in a single block, has been delivered with various resident amenities, along with a nursery, retail and commercial spaces fronting a new public square. The square includes new frontage to the Grand Union Canal, and a new footbridge to link to the wider masterplan. This upfront investment in a fantastic public realm helps establish a community from the outset as well as incorporating site-wide services in an energy centre, which will provide heat and power to the entire masterplan as it is completed. Greystar will retain ownership of the site and Build to Rent buildings and will manage the facilities into the future via an on-site team of full-time community managers.

A BREAK WITH TRADITION

Block 5, now known as Tillermans Court, is the first of seven residential buildings to be completed in early 2020. It is mostly six storeys with a 14-storey corner tower designed to be visible from Greenford Station to the south, and mark the new Grenan Square, overlooking the Grand Union Canal as it snakes east towards central London. The 379 homes contained within the building all share a single main entrance, accessed from the main square, into a generous, double-height space to form a grand entrance. External materials and detailing were worked from a deliberately simple yet robust palette, to create an enduring backdrop for the emerging public realm. The building form creates sunny, west-facing courtyards, and places primary frontages to benefit from views over amenity spaces. The sensitive, biophilic landscape will help foster a feeling of community established quickly from a previously vacant site.

Internally, the design of the building was driven by the client's exacting requirements and operational strategies to create an efficient building to manage while ensuring that every single home has generous space standards, good levels of daylight and a great aspect. Customers seeking to rent a home there have a choice of orientation, views and levels of amenity to suit their lifestyle and budget with discounted affordable homes all sharing the same high standard of provision.

The plan arrangement reflects the aspiration that residents will make use of the many facilities, and live in the building, as much as they do in their apartment. The level of amenities require the building to be intensively managed and accordingly it has been designed to make management as easy as possible. A single main entrance is formed from a large double height space, combined with concierge, parcel and post collection, along with homeworking and lounge space for use by residents. Apartments are accessed by shared cores and corridors sharing some of the characteristics of a hotel, albeit with corridors as wide as 1.8m, facilitating the easy movement of people and furniture, with windows at key corners and end points to provide plenty of natural light. There is a high level of repetition throughout the residential areas while complementary uses are grouped together elsewhere around the building. Clearly the building departs from some of the recommendations of the customary planning expectations in London, with many more apartments around each core than would normally be expected for a private sale or affordable rent scheme. This is driven by considerable experience of successful models of rented 'multi-family' housing in the USA, and is designed to facilitate a higher quality of apartment and increased provision of amenities and facilities.

MODULAR DELIVERY

Initially the intention had been to construct Tillermans based on a traditional reinforced *in-situ* concrete frame, and detailed design had been well progressed for this before a review was undertaken at the end of Stage 3. The procurement and construction approach was subject to a review at a point when Greystar's student living business, Chapter, had completed a number of modular buildings and therefore had gained an appreciation of the potential benefits to the building and to their business. A period of review involving Tide Construction and Vision Modular Systems working with HTA was able to demonstrate that the building would require only relatively minor revisions to facilitate modular delivery. This included incorporating a supersized corner module that rotated orientation at different heights across the building, and clever manipulation of storey heights within a mezzanine workspace, with a stepped transfer slab. With the majority of design issues resolved, Tide were contracted to deliver the project using their sister company Vision Modular Systems. Unusually but reflecting the keenness to ensure a successful outcome, the architecture team at HTA who had undertaken the design up to the end of Stage 3, retained a role as part of the client monitoring team, while a separate team at HTA with considerable experience of modular construction having already completed six projects with Tide Construction and Vision, were engaged to deliver Stage 4 working drawings through the construction phase to completion.

Construction of Tillermans along with the energy centre, public realm and bridge over the canal, commenced in June 2018 was completed in February 2020, a construction period of just 20 months for 379 homes. The construction sequence is based on a traditional foundation and superstructure package up to a first floor transfer slab with six cores rising

Fig 4
A view taken during construction showing the slip-formed core and some of the modules installed

Fig 5
A view of the construction after all modules were installed and the cladding partially completed

up to various heights at each corner of the E-shaped building. The concrete has to be finished to incredibly high tolerances to accommodate the precision engineered modules. Vision's system is based on a hot rolled steel-framed module with a slim concrete slab cast into the modular frame to provide a robust construction that also helps achieve the required fire and noise separation between apartment floors.

Module installation can commence prior to completion of the *in-situ* concrete works, with careful management of crane time, and the availability of a large site enabled modules to be delivered in advance of being required to enable installations to continue according to availability and to suit conditions. Modules are delivered to site with mechanical and electrical fittings, kitchens, bathrooms, decorations and windows already installed and with rooms fully watertight.

The facade works were also started prior to completion of the module installation, being independent of internal finishing as modules are all delivered to site fully watertight. This ability to continue multiple operations concurrently reduces the number of activities forming part of a critical path, helping to reduce potential delays to programme through any particular individual package of works.

MEASURING THE BENEFITS

The project has further demonstrated a wide range of benefits of modular delivery for a Build to Rent developer and operator such as Greystar, including:

- Speed of construction – much quicker period on site (up to 50%), allowing earlier completion and lease-up of new homes and quicker repayment of financing costs.
- Consistency of quality control – as most fit-out works are completed before the modules reach site, quality of the product is 'right first time' and durable and on-site snagging and defects are minimised helping to reduce longer term maintenance costs.

- Design efficiencies – details such as the slender party wall construction that still achieves full acoustic separation result in enhanced lettable area, with a total net area increase of around 8% gained in the transfer from traditional to modular construction.
- Cost certainty – an efficient and stable modular supply chain, together with reduced dependence upon site-based labour, results in better financial control and cost certainty.
- Positive impact on placemaking – completing buildings and open space quickly helps establish a place early in the process of development and increases the appeal to customers as a place to live.
- Reduced disruption – vehicle movements for on-site deliveries were reduced by around 80% compared with traditional build, with less noise and dust helping to minimise the impact on the existing nearby community, while also improving conditions for new residents as later phases are delivered.

The project demonstrates the compatibility of modular construction for delivering purpose designed and built, professionally managed housing for rent, as higher standards of finish, reduced defects and much earlier completion can easily offset the potentially higher costs of building this way. The project also demonstrates that although the modular component is a substantial part of the project, coordination with the traditional elements of construction is critical to achieving a beneficial outcome. It is as critical that the contractor can effectively manage the interface between concrete structure and modules, and between modules and facades and finishing, where the game can potentially be lost, however high quality and quick the modules may be.

Indeed, many benefits were brought to the delivery of the project through the inherently open-minded attitude towards innovation and problem solving that a manufacturing company can bring even to traditional construction. With floor 14 of the tower designated as amenity space for residents, a large clear span space not best suited to modular construction as desired by the Greystar design team. To achieve this, the modular 13th floor was capped with another concrete slab cast on site in pieces within prefabricated steel frames and craned up to form an entire floor. The steel superstructure was then prefabricated and also assembled on site while a proprietary concrete floor was added for enhanced acoustic insulation between the gym, cinema, residents' entertainment lounge and the residential apartments. This hybrid approach was a first for the team and required a high level of coordination but continued the process of shared learning, which was further advanced for future projects with similar requirements.

RESPONDING TO A CHANGING REGULATORY ENVIRONMENT

While factory-made modular construction demands a shift in approach to design and decision making to be conducted much earlier in the design process, the modular construction method also demonstrated its potential dexterity during the construction process. New building regulations emerged during construction which focused on fire spread in high-rise buildings. Although not a requirement to meet new regulations given construction was already underway, Vision was able to review alternative modular panels, carry out testing and offer a revised build-up to satisfy the new requirements without compromising any of the design parameters already set and agreed. Despite the rapid speed of build it was agreed that the

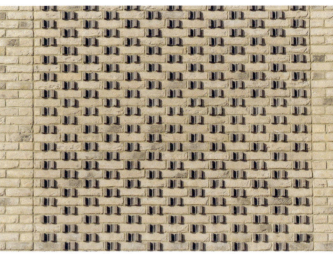

new compliant approach would be adopted for the long-term benefit of the project, and was a mutually beneficial revision for both client and manufacturer.

A further complexity of apartment construction using volumetric modules is that services and ventilation systems need to connect between modules and are not just connected to the communal systems through the end of the module into the corridors. This requires more work within the modules than usually happens in hotel or student accommodation construction and creates some requirement for additional protection and cleaning within the module before handover.

Modules for Greenford were constructed off site by Vision Modular Systems Ltd, from their Bedford factory, generating 80% less material waste of which 97% is recycled. The factory provides a clean and safe environment for a locally based workforce, a majority of which are able to cycle to work.

AN INTEGRATED DESIGN APPROACH

As well as the architecture and landscape design HTA developed production information for the interior design and wayfinding developed from a concept by interior designers Woods Bagot, and integrated into the architectural model through to final detailing. The interdisciplinary approach to design with a single organisation providing coordinated design information in a single BIM model is of crucial benefit to ensuring timely input and sign-off from the client team. The final design result of the client's brief is a simple rational building created from high-quality materials and components sitting in a rich, biophilic landscape.

The masterplan, the buildings and the public realm all aim to create bright and liveable apartments with great facilities and within a beautiful landscape. As the building is for rent, the apartments are effectively on sale many times during their lifetime meaning they need to be welcoming and spacious with good views and amenities to set them apart from other homes available on the market and ensure they are never vacant for long.

The design team have worked hard to make a complex building simple, and kept the building exterior and plan in sync with each other, reaching a high level of external simplicity which hides a well-worked plan. The building reflects its use insofar as the high-quality interiors, complex mix of resident amenities and concierge team are made possible by the scale of the building. Traditional buildings for sale or for affordable rental tend to keep the common parts small to reduce management costs. The strategy here instead is to make the common parts accessible to the highest number of people. All the tenants' rental costs are covering the costs of the services to ensure a high level of service can be afforded and available to everyone living in the building.

The first residents moved in just 16 months after works commenced on site with a phased handover that led to completion four months later. Greystar intend to complete the entire project within around seven years – much less than half the time a similar traditional market sale and affordable housing scheme might achieve and with the considerable additional benefits set out above.

Greenford is the first Build to Rent project that Greystar and Tide Construction are delivering via modular construction and follows three previous modular student housing developments on which the two companies have collaborated. Once complete, it will bring

Fig 6 (top left)
The completed building showing the ordered facade and the relationship between the taller corner and the neighbouring lower range

Fig 7 (top right)
A close-up of the brickwork cladding showing the careful detailing

Fig 8 (middle left)
A close-up of the facade showing a typical residential balcony and the brickwork quality

Fig 9 (bottom left)
The stepped landscaped leading from the canal to the central square fronting Tillermans

Fig 10 (bottom right)
A view along Grand Union Canal

Fig 11
The building's reception area

Fig 12
Ground floor workspace with bespoke joinery

Fig 13
14th floor private dining and commercial kitchen for residents to book

the total number of units the partnership has delivered in London so far to 1600 units. This demonstrates that volumetric modular will play a central role in the future of residential construction and Greystar is already benefiting from being an early adopter.

James Pargeter, Senior Director, Projects at Greystar Europe said: 'We have an amazing opportunity to revitalise this previously neglected site in Greenford to create a new mixed-use canalside neighbourhood which is strong and inclusive, with placemaking at its heart.'[1]

Fig 14
The development under progress viewed from a distance

Fig 15
Residents moving in

FACTS

Location	Greenford Quay, Tillermans Court, Greenford Road, Greenford, London UB6 0HE
Planning authority	London Borough of Ealing
Client	Greystar
Main contractor	Tide Construction Ltd
Modular manufacturer	Vision Modular Systems
Modular construction	Steel-framed with concrete floor
Architect	HTA Design LLP
Type of housing	Build to Rent apartments, nursery and commercial
Start date	June 2018
Completion date	February 2020
Construction period	20 months
Number of homes	379 homes
Number of modules	1180 modules
Number of storeys	14 and 6
Site area	Masterplan area = 8.64ha
Operator	Greystar

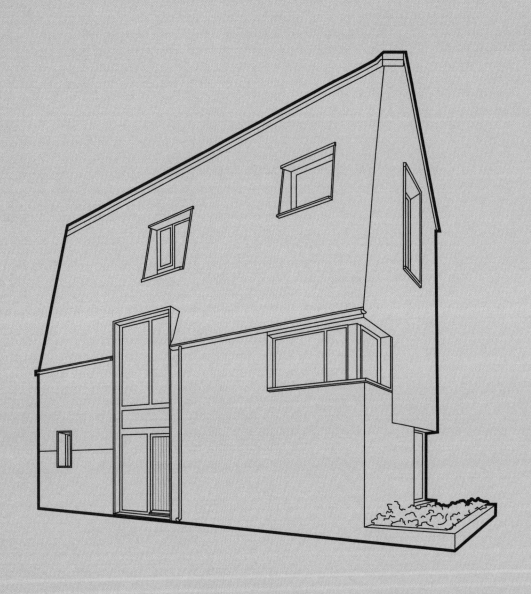

Case Study 4: Beechwood West, Basildon

At Beechwood West, Swan Housing Association's landmark regeneration of the 1960's Craylands Estate, a uniquely customisable new neighbourhood harnesses all the benefits of modular construction.

Alongside development partners Basildon Borough Council and the Homes and Communities Agency, Swan/NU Living and architects PTE have responded to the government's new custom-build and self-build initiatives to design 251 new homes that residents can personalise to their own requirements and tastes, creating a unique home that they have helped to design.

 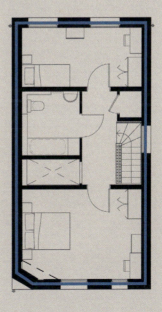 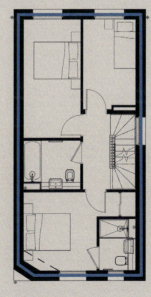

Fig 1 (facing)
Line drawing of a Beechwood West House

Fig 2
Floor plan and modular layout

House Types		
	House Type	Count
	Park Corner	1
	Lane	36
	Terrace	63
	Avenue Semi Detached	74
	Avenue Detached	43
	Park Corner	18
	Fryth	8
	Self Build	9
Grand Total:		252

 NHS Building

Fig 3
A visualisation of the completed development

Fig 4
Development layout of the different house types

Buyers of new homes in Britain lament the lack of choice, especially in low-value areas where cost tends to drive out character. By contrast this project offers customers the chance to design their own homes and achieves cost effectiveness through offsite factory production. The client, Swan, saw the opportunity for personalisation, from the room layout through to the external finishes and internal specification, as a unique prospect for buyers including those with a first-time buyer budget. This was one of the key reasons for choosing to use modular construction.

HOW DOES IT WORK?

Potential buyers can design their new home via an online configurator; with five starter houses to choose from, residents first select their plot and then create their new homes using specialist sales software. Starting with the basics – number of bedrooms, arrangement of the downstairs and upstairs plans and the level of specification; residents can then choose from a palette of external finishes for walls, roofs and windows and even add bays, conservatories or roof extensions. The framework of choices available has been carefully selected to ensure that each home is unique, but that their variety adds to the interest of the finished streets. The smart menu of custom-build options amounts to a million combinations.

CONTEXT AND QUALITY

A custom-build approach to delivery of the new homes requires the materials to be not only robust and attractive, but also cohesive and completely interchangeable.

Drawing its inspiration from the best of British suburban housing, Beechwood West is steeped in the Arts and Crafts attention to detail that is so sought after today, while still remaining contemporary in appearance and boasting 21st-century environmental performance.

The framework of choices available was carefully selected to ensure that each home is unique and that the potential variety generated would achieve a quintessentially 'suburban' appearance. By varying the building form, typology, scale and density of the proposal, the development creates places of different character and interest which respond sensitively to the existing landscape edges.

The house types have been organised into three distinct families, with a primary avenue fronted by two-storey, three- and four-bed detached and semi-detached houses. The secondary north–south streets are lined with continuous two-, three- and four-bed terrace houses. Two-bed lane houses, which line tertiary streets to the south-west and north-east, create a third distinct character area. All homes create clearly defined edges to public spaces and encourage natural surveillance while still allowing for a defensible edge to delineate public and private space.

Fig 5
Two bedroom terraced houses set along mews style streets

Fig 6
Homes showing the variation of materials stemming from residents' choices

PLANNING

Modular construction was considered from an early stage in the design process; the team consulted regularly with Basildon Borough Council throughout 2015 and 2016 to agree how best to enable the custom-build aspirations for the site while still ensuring a high-quality and coherent new neighbourhood would be delivered.

The project aimed to positively encourage the suburban phenomenon of individualisation, allowing each resident to express their own choices. But to give the local authority confidence that variety would create a positive result as opposed to a chaotic neighbourhood character, the designers rendered the same views of different streets with completely different combinations of the agreed material palette. As a result, the planning officers agreed that it was the extent of variation that actually gave the project its interest and distinctive qualities.

A hybrid application for the development was submitted in May of 2016 with all matters submitted in detail except for appearance, and a detailed Design Code was submitted with the application, outlining the design standards that would be applicable to all future reserved matters applications for each individual plot. This code gave clear guidance to stakeholders, designers, developers, contractors and the local planning authority on how to deliver a consistent, high-quality and coherent neighbourhood that would still maximise flexibility and customisation for its future inhabitants. Resolution to grant planning consent was approved on 5 September 2016.

CASE STUDY 4: BEECHWOOD WEST, BASILDON

Fig 7
A house module being manufactured in the Swan NU Build's factory

Fig 8
Modules arriving on site for installation

CONSTRUCTION

The project is currently under construction with the new homes being pre-constructed as modular, cross-laminated timber (CLT) pods, in a factory close to the site, utilising local labour. They are transported to the site and erected on the plot before being finished by an on-site team. Compared to the traditional delivery of housing, this methodology provides purchasers with benefits including a high quality controlled finish, energy efficiencies from constructional accuracy, minimised impact of construction on neighbouring residents, and extensive time savings from purchase to moving in.

CHALLENGES

While the extent of custom variety is one of the assets, it also brings design, management and constructional challenges. PTE worked closely with Swan's sales team to agree how a matrix of a million choices would be communicated to potential buyers, as well as with the manufacturing team, to understand the expected sequence of trades.

There are certainly design challenges involved in this level of mass-customisation. For example, the extent of drawing management is greatly increased when offering such a breadth of options to the buyer. Each possible design configuration needs to be fully tested, and to ensure this is possible, the entire consultant team worked in Revit to a BIM Level 2.

Though there are barriers to making custom-building a more mainstream system, we are certainly in an era where the design of homes is in the mainstream consciousness. The problem is the disconnect between a design savvy generation and their ability to raise funds to purchase a new home.

PTE see the swell of volumetric housing solutions now coming to the market, including from the major housebuilders, as being an opportunity to offer more choice to buyers, and create better homes for end users.

Geoff Pearce, Executive Director Development and Regeneration, Swan commented: 'Swan is truly committed to delivering innovation. Offsite construction is commonly used overseas and the homes are indistinguishable from ones that are built using more traditional methods. We already have our own in-house skilled construction team and so, as both the constructor and developer of the homes, we are perfectly placed to manage the process of building homes offsite efficiently and to the highest standards.'

Duncan Hayes, Editor of *Custom Build Strategy* said: 'This is custom build innovation in action. On one side PTE has developed a formula for customising at scale, offering a million choices on a large site, supported by a digitised process. But the concept of customised home is being used at Beechwood West as a marketing tool to create interest and demand, attracting residents that might not otherwise consider the development. Clever stuff indeed.'

FACTS

Location	Beechwood West, Basildon, Essex, SS14 3RN
Planning authority	Basildon Borough Council
Client	Swan Housing Association
Main contractor	NU Living
Modular manufacturer	NU Living / NU Build
Modular construction	Cross-laminated timber
Architect	Pollard Thomas Edwards
Type of housing	Suburban low rise
Start date	November 2016
Completion date	Under construction
Number of homes	251 homes
Number of modules	Over 1000
Number of storeys	2 and 3
Site area	8ha
Operator	Swan Housing Association

Figs 9, 10
Completed homes ready to be sold and occupied

Fig 11
A visualisation of the completed development

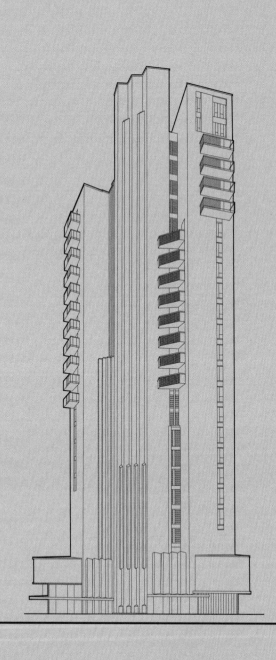

Case Study 5: Mapleton Crescent, Wandsworth, London

Jonathan Drage, Dhruv Sookhoo and Neil Deely

Mapleton Crescent, Wandsworth, is Pocket Living's first high-rise modular building and on completion was the tallest residential modular construction in Europe.[1] That Pocket Living has gone on to develop a second high-rise modular project at Addiscombe Grove in Croydon also designed by Metropolitan Workshop is evidence of growing confidence in the ability of volumetric, modular construction to fulfil the objectives of expanding residential programmes by clients seeking enhanced cost certainty, improved build quality and timely delivery.

Fig 1 (facing)
Line drawing of Mapleton Crescent

Fig 2
Floor plan and modular layout

183

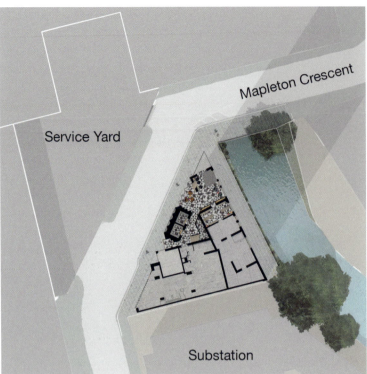

Fig 3
River Wandle view

Fig 4
Site plan

The project is also evidence that modular projects are enabling increased design quality with the architectural critic, Rowan Moore commenting: 'This stylish new 27-storey residential tower is an exemplar of innovative modular housing ... It has a pleasantly slender profile, with shifting rhythms and a nice balance of verticals and horizontals. The textured surfaces of the faience give a sense of depth and liveliness you don't get in most cladding systems ... Modular units are used not as prophecy but as the best available means in a given circumstance. It must be said that this project is singular.'[2]

Mapleton Crescent offers insight into how volumetric construction can help to optimise site capacity of an irregular shaped site, to realise a programme of affordable homes enriched by generous social spaces. The 27-storey tower provides 89 apartments, constructed from steel-framed volumetric modules and supported by a concrete platform and core. This hybrid approach reflects design decision-making concerning the need to address demanding site-specific constraints and respond creatively to interpret a new high-rise model for affordable housing offered by Pocket Living. In addition to considering site and programmatic issues, the project aimed to create a material language capable of representing a positive reading of place, on an apparently unprepossessing site within a rapidly changing neighbourhood. This less tangible objective resulted in what is arguably Mapleton Crescent's defining feature: its lustrous, pleated, ceramic turquoise facade.

Mapleton Crescent was adapted for modular construction from a traditional concrete frame during a period of intense post-tender collaboration with Tide Construction Ltd and Vision Modular Systems (Vision). The resulting proposal combined the efficiencies available

Fig 5
Construction sequence

through modular construction for replicable home types with a structural concrete platform and stair core necessary to address complex site constraints and produce a sociable entrance level. The construction of the concrete base and load-transfer frame, and slipform concrete core took five months and six weeks respectively. The factory-built volumetric modules incorporating apartments and sections of the common corridor were craned into position within eight weeks, at the rate of just over one floor per day. The pace and precision offered by modular construction aided site operations within a context defined by proximity to a busy road, river and neighbouring buildings by minimising delivery traffic and reducing the number of tradespeople at risk within a congested site. Modular construction reduced waste on site, offered a higher quality finish than traditional construction and enhanced programme certainty. Pocket Living have received positive qualitative feedback from their customers about the design and construction quality of the finished project.[3]

Pocket Living originally commissioned Metropolitan Workshop to develop a proposal to optimise the capacity of a highly constrained, long-neglected small site perceived by others as potentially undevelopable.[4] The triangular plot is defined by the River Wandle to the east, a primary electricity substation to the south and is encircled by the Southside Shopping Centre and attendant service yards and multi-storey car parking [Figure 2]. The context of several tall buildings of up to 25 storeys on neighbouring sites provided a precedent and reflects Wandsworth Council's support for tall appropriate buildings of high design quality contributing to social inclusion and economic vitality through new affordable housing.

DESIGN DEVELOPMENT

The eastern 25-storey stack is orientated to capture riverside views and accommodate three space standard compliant Pocket Homes per floor, transitioning to a pair of two-bedroom three-person private sale apartments on the twelfth floor. The southern 27-storey stack accommodates a pair of space standard compliant Pocket Homes per floor, transitioning to provide a single three-bedroom five-person private sale apartment per floor [Figure 6].

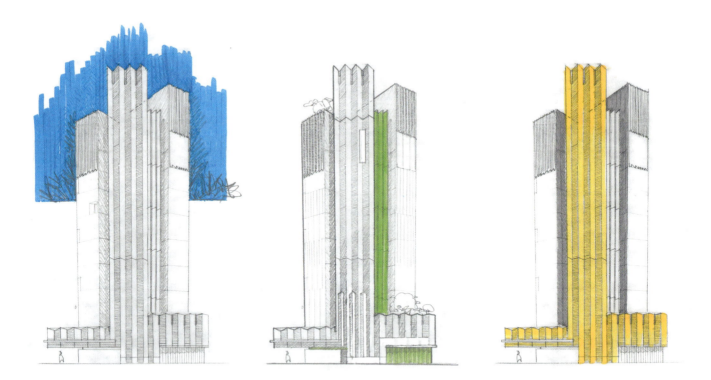

Fig 6
Early project sketches

The core was orientated to the north-western boundary as the shopping centre offered low visual amenity. Extending the slender core vertically above apartment stacks sheltered a south-easterly facing roof terrace [Figure 7]. Internally, the arrangement contributes to naturally lit and ventilated corridors and ensures two thirds of apartments are dual-aspect or triple-aspect. Single-aspect apartments are south or east facing thereby maximising lighting levels because of Pocket's insistence on floor to ceiling windows. This arrangement accommodated 53 affordable Pocket Homes and 36 larger private sale Pocket Edition apartments.[5]

Pocket Living's post-planning decision to adopt volumetric modular construction for Mapleton Crescent was informed by their experience of enhanced cost certainty, improved build quality and quicker than anticipated completion times at Mount Earl Gardens, Streatham by HKR Architects. This success coincided with a tender process for Mapleton Crescent which saw the selection of Donban and Vision over contractors proposing traditional concrete frames. As the project progressed, the developer became determined to challenge the assumption that modular construction can only produce viable, efficient and liveable solutions within regular, unconstrained conditions. In a sense the modular construction was co-opted into a wider mission to prove the unpromising site developable.

Pocket Living agreed to fund Donban through part release of the contract sum to establish compatibility in principle, resulting in the decision to construct the lower floors and central core in concrete and upper floors using modular construction. Once compatibility had been established the design and build contract was signed with Metropolitan Workshop being novated to the contractor and the structural engineer remaining on the client-side to

CASE STUDY 5: MAPLETON CRESCENT, WANDSWORTH, LONDON

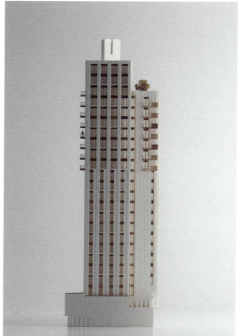
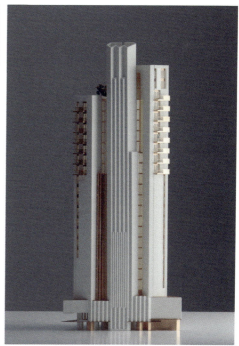

Fig 7
Model – south view

Fig 8
Model – north-west view

verify ongoing structural design development and coordination. Requirements for additional roof slab thickness for wind effect mitigation, shallower floor-to-floor heights permitted by modular construction, a 1.5m thick transfer slab and extra concrete for the special crane above the lifts only resulted in an increase to the overall building height of a few hundred millimetres.

OFFSITE MANUFACTURER OF STEEL MODULES

Vision Modular Systems were responsible for manufacturing the 243 volumetric steel modules required to complete Mapleton Crescent from their factory in Luton, Bedfordshire. A typical one-bedroom Pocket Home was fabricated from two volumetric modules, with all modules being fabricated in approximately three months. Interior finishes, services, kitchens and bathrooms and windows are installed before the module is sealed within weather resistant boards within the factory to allow outdoor storage before transportation and on-site assembly. Vision can complete an entire module within 12 days. Vision is a member of the Buildoffsite Property Assurance Scheme (BOPAS) and provides British Board of Agrément (BBA) certification, proving competence and fitness for purpose with a typical lifespan of 60 years.

Fig 9
Ceramic test panels for cladding

CONSTRUCTION SEQUENCE

The concrete base, ground-floor slab and three lower floors of the load-transfer frame were completed within five months, by March 2017 [Figure 5 (b)]. Concurrently Metropolitan Workshop, Vision and their consultants finalised the detailed design of the steel modules. The triangular concrete core was completed within six weeks using pneumatically assisted slipformed concrete construction. Once the slipform core was complete the slipform working platform and tower crane were removed via a mobile crane from Mapleton Crescent. A road closure was required to use the mobile crane to assemble a large crane on top of the lift shaft [Figure 5 (c)]. Individual modules weighed up to 10t and their widths were kept at around 3.4m to allow for road widths and enable ready transportation by lorry without police escort. All modules were installed within two months, roof slabs were craned into position and cladding commenced on the eastern elevation [Figure 5 (e)]. Eight mast-climbing work platforms between 5 and 12m long were used during the installation of the ceramic cladding to enable simultaneous access to multiple floors. Due to site constraints scaffolding platforms were cantilevered over the River Wandle to support cladding of the eastern elevation. With cladding near complete and balconies in position the tower crane was removed by mobile crane and three layers of prefabricated steelwork were concurrently positioned over the lift shafts to construct the distinctive form of the higher central core [Figure 5 (c)].

Construction was completed within a 20-month build programme and achieved construction costs around 10% and 15% lower using modular construction than if the building had been constructed using a concrete frame.[6] Volumetric construction reduced site waste and storage on a constrained site and limited the volume and frequency of deliveries and

Fig 10
View of the ground floor lobby

potential road closures. Constructing the project using modular technology helped achieve a 37% reduction in carbon dioxide emissions. These readily measurable outcomes at the project level have supported the case for adoption of modular construction across Pocket Living's programme with potential to offer benefits through economies in construction and use associated with replicable house types. Mapleton Crescent demonstrates the capacity of volumetric modular construction to contribute to design and development strategies able to unlock even the most constrained, small urban sites to enhance the supply of quality housing in the UK. While there is need to build an evidence base about the consumer experiences of residents living in modular homes to inform improvements in design and construction, there is little evidence of an aversion to living within a volumetrically constructed home at Mapleton Crescent. In a recent BBC London (2019) interview, Mapleton Crescent residents emphasised the pleasure of using the communal social spaces to work and meet friends and the light, spacious feel of their apartment.[7] Tellingly, one resident chose to focus on the spaciousness of her apartment, explaining that if she had not been told her home was produced using modular construction she would not have realised. As Rowan Moore (2018) describes, it is the unnoticed quality of the modular construction at Mapleton Crescent that is its strength.[8] Modular construction inconspicuously solves problems and helped enable the more visible realisation of more profound design objectives: generating a material response to place able to enrich the public realm, articulating sociable shared interior spaces to foster a sense of community, and honing the design of individual dwellings to add economy and joy to the lives of hardworking Londoners. These are lessons that Metropolitan Workshop have taken to the next high-rise modular project for Pocket at Addiscombe Grove, Croydon, and to other modular residential projects in development that are part of a growing realisation about the potential of modular construction to support new forms of architecture.

CASE STUDY 5: MAPLETON CRESCENT, WANDSWORTH, LONDON

Fig 11 (facing)
Folded ceramics of the core meeting the street

Fig 12
Residents' lounge

FACTS

Location	11 Mapleton Crescent, Wandsworth, London, SW18 4AU
Planning authority	Wandsworth London Borough Council
Client	Pocket Living
Main contractor	Tide Construction Ltd
Modular manufacturer	Vision Modular Systems
Module construction	Steel frame and concrete composite module
Architect	Metropolitan Workshop
Type of housing	Pocket Homes
Start date	October 2016
Completion date	June 2018
Construction period	22 months
Number of homes	89
Number of modules	243
Number of storeys	27
Operator	N/A

Case Study 6:
Union Wharf, Greenwich

Union Wharf is a pioneering 249-home Build to Rent development that includes an array of residents' amenities and an extensive public realm along Deptford Creek located near Greenwich town centre and the Cutty Sark DLR station.

The scheme has established many precedents in the Build to Rent sector; it includes the UK's first private rented building specifically designed for families; it successfully challenged the London Plan's balcony provision in favour of shared amenity spaces by creating oversized apartments with the balcony space added to the floor area and providing communal amenities; it is one of the first high-rise residential projects in the UK to use volumetric offsite construction; and it pioneered the concept of discount market rent (DMR) as the affordable contribution.

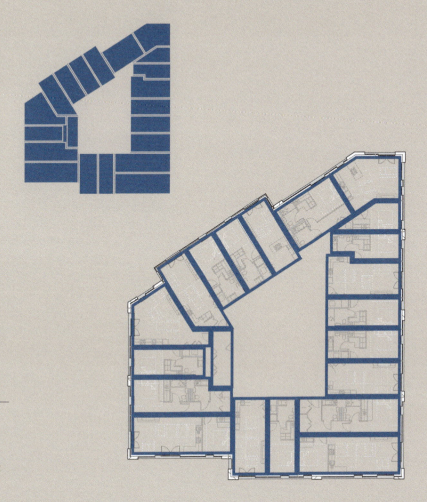

Fig 1 (facing)
Line drawing of Union Wharf

Fig 2
Floor plan and modular layout

Fig 3
Union Wharf seen from Deptford Creek

Fig 4
Looking west over Creek Road Bridge

These DMR homes are pepper-potted across the two buildings to create an entirely tenure-blind development. Union Wharf is now used as a case study industry-wide and was cited in the government's Housing White Paper.[1]

Residents' amenity plays an integral role in Union Wharf's design, ensuring the home begins when entering the building, starting at ground floor with a large lobby, concierge and café, and extending to roof level where communal dining areas, lounges, exercise space and pizza ovens help to build a strong community feeling.

With 72% of the site occupied by public realm, the development opens up to the wider community; including children's play space and a nursery and Creek Walk designed for pop-up markets to reinvigorate and celebrate the waterside location.

The 10-storey 'family' building comprises 60 two and three-bedroom dual-aspect apartments that feature large balconies designed to enhance child safety and high acoustic insulation to cater for early bed times. Communal areas have additional storage for pushchairs and scooters, wider corridors are buggy-friendly and an amenity-focused rooftop floor provides children's play space, grow-your-own allotment gardens, a lounge and games room, a 'workshop' for messy school projects, and a hireable space for socials and children's parties, all designed to meet the specific needs of families. This building is complemented by the new nursery that offers families on-site childcare.

This building exemplifies how Build to Rent design principles can be broadened beyond a narrow perception of the market to meet the needs of a diverse range of residents, whether families with young children, 'empty nest' downsizers or the older, retired generations. With loneliness a major problem, intergenerational Build to Rent developments can foster new communities for 'later living', and key elements of the family building can be applied to these schemes: oversized lifts suitable for wheelchairs, larger apartments for those who prefer to stay home, and ample storage for bicycles, mobility scooters and a lifetime of personal artefacts.

Measures were integrated into the design to enable Essential Living to successfully manage the development over the long term. These include dedicated back-of-house areas with storage for the many daily parcel deliveries, CHP plant to provide low-carbon heat and power, refuse chutes for waste and recycling, a high level of component and layout standardisation and robust material specification.

The rationalisation of design elements, coupled with a repeated floorplate and Build to Rent principles such as equal bedroom sizes in apartments, presented the opportunity to apply a modular method of construction and, at 23 storeys, the development is now one of the tallest volumetric residential buildings in the country. The 635 offsite manufactured fully fitted modules, installed at a rate of one floor per week, offered a potential saving in construction programme, enhanced quality assurance and reduced noise on site to benefit the surrounding community. Assael has collaborated with HTA Design throughout the detailed design process.

This was Essential Living's first foray into the world of modular construction, and their first use of a construction management approach to delivering a project. This led to a complex and unusual delivery mechanism which may have contributed to the building not being much quicker to finish than a traditional one. The construction management team InnC was set up to deliver the project which it did successfully and was then wound up on completion. InnC was a joint venture set up between the client and the modular manufacturer and aimed to fulfil the role usually occupied by a main contractor, but in this case comprised a team who procured and managed all the construction packages needed to deliver the building. It is an example of the potential delivery mechanisms that may become used to delivery prefabricated buildings as clients move away from the traditional contracting model of design and build. The potential benefit of this approach is that there is a regular close relationship between the client and the manufacturer who delivers the bulk of the project in terms of value.

The building was delivered by a trio of companies who would normally work under a main contractor. Elements Europe supplied the roof, volumetric modules and the prefabricated balconies. Conneely supplied and installed the facade and the balconies. O'Keefe carried out the piling, slipform cores and other groundworks. InnC were responsible for tendering these packages and managing the coordination and installation of them to completion. They handled all the project construction finances to completion on behalf of the client.

The building had been designed to RIBA Stage 4 when Essential Living took the decision to change from traditional construction to volumetric modular due to difficulty in sourcing a traditional contractor for the project. HTA Design and Assael collaborated from that point on to deliver the building. A tender process was held to identify the modular supplier and Elements Europe were the successful tenderer and delivered the bulk of the project construction including all modular works and the facade.

As the building had been designed around repetitive layouts for the rental market it was relatively easy to convert the design from traditional construction to volumetric modular. The floor plans repeated vertically through each building, ensuring load paths and service routes stacked neatly above each other. HTA successfully realised the modularisation of the apartments and divided the layouts into modules working alongside Elements Europe and their design team. The apartments were divided into module-sized rooms and arranged around a reinforced concrete core which was built traditionally using slipform construction.

One significant change from the Stage 3 design was that the reinforced concrete core was enlarged to encompass the residential corridors to provide greater structural stability and reduce the number of module-to-module connections in the structure.

The volumetric construction approach enabled the client to deliver the project to their high quality standards, using factory production to ensure a high level of finish was achieved throughout the building. Rental projects which are designed to be for rent in perpetuity need to be lettable to new tenants over their lifetime and must be easy to maintain. Factory production enabled the services and finishes to be done in the factory to a large extent and installed consistently throughout the contract.

Adapting the design for a modular construction saw a small increase in gross external area (GEA)/building footprint and a 1.9m increase in height, which the local planning authority had little objection to due to the range of benefits the innovative construction method would bring to the locality of the site.

The volumetric manufacturer rented a short-term facility with a staging area outside London to park modules, temporarily enabling deliveries to be coordinated with site access and ensure a smooth flow of modules to site.

Because most of the site was being built on, the construction management team rented the adjacent site and used it for site offices and accommodation for some of the contract period.

The modular construction was not as smooth as it could have been and did not deliver on the programme advantages originally targeted by the client in part due to a long period of inclement weather. The modular construction led to difficulties in the delivery of the cantilevered balconies and required some on-site remedial work to be implemented. This was exacerbated by the need to use scaffolding to install the Corium brick slip facade system. The scaffolding made it difficult to install the balcony components.

The final building is identical to the design submitted for planning and is a testament to the efforts of the design and construction team. On opening the building was fully let within five months of completion.

The residents are forming an active community using social media to communicate with each other, they hold regular get-togethers for residents, and share tools and equipment.

Residents' feedback is generally positive; one resident interviewed reported that as a resident she feels 'privileged to live in this project since August. The neighbourhood is very well connected and pleasant to live in as is it so close to the River Thames and Ravensbourne. The specifications are good quality and the flat layout (one-bed two-person flat) very pleasant and convenient and we have a good south-west facing view. The thermal comfort brought by the underfloor heating is very good and it can be controlled in each room. There is excellent acoustic insulation as well for both outside noises or neighbours; we never hear the neighbours next door or under/above ... We often use the communal spaces with friends visiting or with neighbours such as the gym, the rooftop or pool table. What's more, the fact that we have all bills including internet, water, heating and electricity included in the rent brings a peace of mind.'

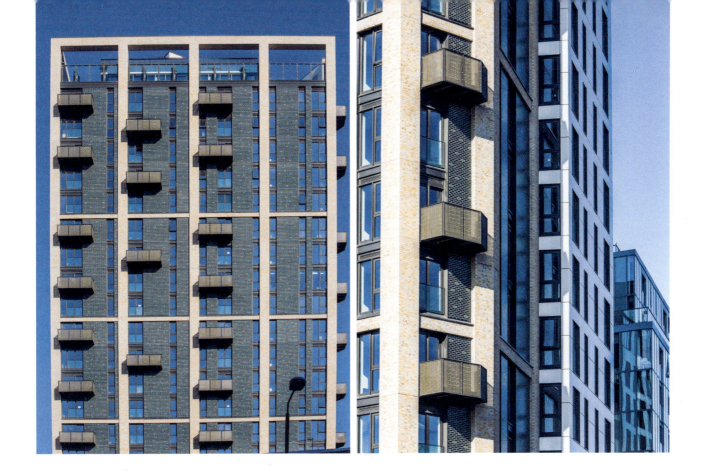

Figs 5, 6
The facade of Union Wharf showing balconies and cladding arrangement

FACTS

Location	Copperas Street, London, SE8 3GS
Planning authority	London Borough of Greenwich
Client	Essential Living
Main contractor	INNC Construction Management
Modular manufacturer	Elements Europe Ltd
Module construction	Steel-framed with steel floor
Architect	Assael (Design)
	HTA Design LLP (Modular design and Delivery)
Type of housing	Build-to-rent high rise
Start date	May 2018
Completion date	December 2019
Construction period	31 months
Number of homes	249 homes
Number of modules	635 modules
Number of storeys	22 and 12
Operator	Essential Living

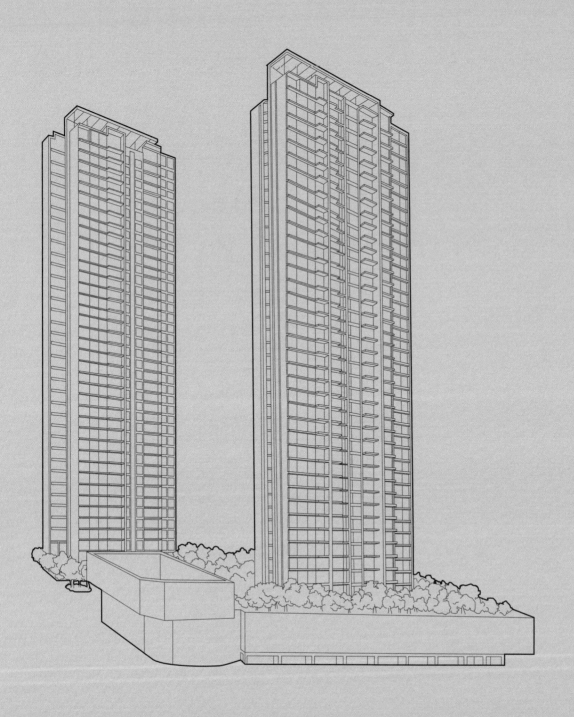

Case Study 7: Clement Canopy, Singapore

Maey Leow

One of the most notable international modular projects of recent years is Clement Canopy in Singapore. Formed of two apartment blocks, each 40 storeys tall, the towers delivered 505 residential apartments above a range of communal facilities including a swimming pool and basement car park, and was finished in early 2019. The development of the Clement Canopy project was a joint venture between Singland Homes Pte Ltd and UOL Group Ltd, which is one of the leading public-listed property companies in Singapore with a diversified portfolio of development and investment properties, hotels and serviced suites.

The project is unique amongst the case studies presented here in being constructed in fully reinforced concrete modules, in what is known locally as precast prefinished volumetric

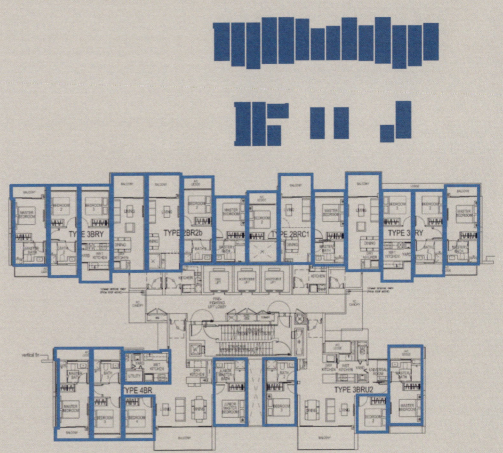

Fig 1 (facing)
Line drawing of Clement Canopy

Fig 2
Floor plan and modular layout

Figs 3, 4
The towers' facades are made from rendered and painted concrete, with aluminium window frames

construction (PPVC). This was driven by an initiative from the Building and Construction Authority (BCA) of Singapore to promote productivity in the construction industry through offsite manufacturing. One of the main goals is to move as much as 90% of typical construction works to a controlled factory environment for all the finishing works and minimise on-site construction. In addition, as part of the Singapore authorities' efforts to encourage offsite construction such as PPVC, the Government Land Sales (GLS) programme mandates that 65% of the superstructure's floor area be built with offsite volumetric construction.

Working in tandem with the authorities, TW-ASIA Consultants Pte Ltd was at the forefront of PPVC development and pioneered the advanced research of the reinforced concrete composite shear wall structural system and submitted for patent the PPVC technology in order to enter the PPVC market. It was through research, testing and continual development that a unique structural system was devised as a technical solution for PPVC construction using a six-sided module that would be manufactured in the factory and delivered to site for assembly.

STRUCTURAL SYSTEM

While the PPVC technology is new to the construction industry at the time of implementation, some of the core engineering principles of structural design, foundation design and superstructure engineering design (lateral stability, ductility, progressive collapse and so on) and compliance with the structural code, remain familiar from conventional construction.

There are two key parts that form the structural system: the foundation and the superstructure. The superstructure comprises the 40-storey-high tower blocks and multi-storey car park. The foundation system for the 40-storey tower blocks comprises bored piles while the foundation system for the podium multi-storey car park comprises jack-in spun piles.

In line with the GLS programme, under the BCA's detail guidelines and buildable scoring system for developers and consultants to comply with, the superstructure system for the

40-storey tower blocks comprises a reinforced concrete PPVC system with more than 65% coverage of the superstructure floor area, while the remaining superstructure area comprises a precast reinforced concrete (RC) floor construction with the minimum of cast in-situ lift core and storey shelter.

PPVC MODULARISATION

Conceptually, the idea was to design the tower to be made of modules which could be assembled on site. So naturally the starting point was to envisage the building as 'Lego blocks' or bite-size modules that could be transportable within Singapore's road systems. The dimensions of each module were controlled by the transportation constraints. Therefore during the early design stage, the initial early involvement with all stakeholders, client, consultants and authorities was important and played a part in the successful implementation of the project. Other considerations included the hoisting weight limit of the tower crane and the access to the construction site which were all studied, planned and not left to chance.

The weight of typical PPVC modules made from precast concrete ranges from 18 to 30t requiring use of specialist cranes. There are in total 1866 PPVC modules for the whole project: 862 in Tower 1 and 1004 in Tower 2.

For this project, the sizes of the PPVC modules are designed to be transportable under the local traffic authorities' guidelines. Care had been taken to avoid the need for a police escort which would inevitably increase cost and take more time. The focus was on a just-in-time delivery where the timing for continuous seamless lifting of modules into place did not disrupt the construction schedule.

Overall, after many studies on cost-benefit analysis and deliberating over various options of the process of manufacturing, a single-minded approach or process was adopted for the PPVC: from concrete carcass to fit-out works carried out in factories, and afterwards assembling and stitching the modules on site with minimum wet work.

PROCESS, FACTORY AND INSTALLATION

The typical PPVC module is a precast six-sided RC module comprising a floor slab, a ceiling slab, two side structural walls and two end non-structural wall/doors. The PPVC concrete carcasses with embedded M&E service pipes were all manufactured in Johor, Malaysia, which is just a stone's throw across the Singapore Causeway. To ensure watertightness, stringent quality checks were put in place. For example an early structural ponding test is carried out at the precast factory to check for watertightness of the concrete floor structures.

The completed PPVC concrete carcasses were then delivered to the fit-out factory in Singapore for architecture finishing (floor finishes, wall finishes, painting, window frames and glazing, doors and wardrobes and cabinets) and M&E fit-out works (water and sanitary pipes, electrical conduits and ducting, electrical sockets and light switches). Waterproofing works were carried out in the fit-out factory in the wet areas; followed by water ponding tests to check for watertightness. The PPVC modules for each residential unit were also checked for trial fitting in the fit-out factory to ensure that the adjoining modules could fit together correctly before delivery to site for final installation.

On site, upon installation of the PPVC modules, the adjoining PPVC modules' walls were joined together with in-situ high-strength grout; resulting in composite structure walls. These PPVC modules are also connected to the balance cast in-situ floor structures and lift core and storey shelter walls to derive the tower lateral-load resisting mechanism for wind load. For this project, the total duration of the PPVC module installation was approximately 12 months; the average floor cycle time was six to nine days. The first two to three floors took a longer cycle time as they were in the initial learning curve of the module installation.

DESIGN BUILDABILITY, CONSTRUCTABILITY AND MANPOWER SAVING AND PRODUCTIVITY

The adoption of PPVC system in this project has achieved a marked improvement in the design buildability, constructability and manpower saving and productivity. In reference to the Singapore BCA's Code of Practice on Buildability, the project has achieved eight points' improvement above the mandated design Buildability (B-Score) and 10 points above the mandated Constructability (C-Score). The project has also achieved more than 60% productivity saving in the manpower on site.

The productivity, site safety and quality of works have vastly improved compared to traditional methods and contributed to the completion of the project well ahead of schedule.

CHALLENGES FACED AND FUTURE OF VOLUMETRIC CONSTRUCTION IN SINGAPORE

One of the main challenges faced during the implementation of such PPVC modularisation projects is the mindsets of stakeholders involved. Unlike conventional projects whereby detailed design decisions on architectural finishes could be decided later, for this project, the early involvement and decision making of all stakeholders on finishes, M&E services and carpentry works is the key to the PPVC project's success. Because the works are now carried out in the factory much earlier similar to a manufacturing process and brought to site for assembly there is no opportunity to leave those decisions to later in the process.

During the factory fabrication process, much attention has to be given to testing such as pre-assembly trial areas where the cast modules are assembled on the floor as per the tower footprint to ensure the overall alignment of the building. Checks are made that structural verticality, levelness and precise accuracy of the structural connections are in order so that the PPVC modules when sent to the site will fit exactly as per design and the robustness and structural integrity of the building is not compromised in any way.

In Singapore where there is high population density, there is a need to reduce reliance on foreign labour. In order to achieve this objective without compromising on quality and speed of construction, the implementation of offsite PPVC modularisations to construction projects which enhances environmental impact and workers' safety is proving to be a viable solution. There is no doubt that in the near future, many projects will be constructed in such a manner and it will be a new norm in the building and construction industry.

Fig 5 (top left)
A long distance view of the Clement Canopy towers

Fig 6 (top right)
A view of the towers from the base

Fig 7 (bottom left)
A close view of the towers post completion

FACTS

Location	Lot 05327T Mk 03, Clementi Avenue 1, Singapore
Planning authority	Urban Redevelopment Authority
Client	United Venture Development (Clementi) Pte Ltd
Contractor	Dragages Singapore Pte Ltd
Modular manufacturer	Dragages Singapore Pte Ltd
Module construction	Reinforced precast concrete
Architect	ADDP Architects LLP
Start date	June 2016
Completion date	March 2019
Construction period	28 months
Number of homes	505 apartments
Number of modules	1899
Number of storeys	40
Site area	45,633sqm
Operator	N/A

Case Study 8: George Street, Croydon, London

101 George Street is the development of two interconnected residential towers rising to 38 storeys and 44 storeys to an overall height of 135m. The building provides 546 new homes, of which 109 are offered as affordable housing, designed for build-to-rent provider Greystar. The site marks the gateway to the London Borough of Croydon's comprehensive plans for a new 'Cultural Quarter' opposite East Croydon station, and a high level of design ambition

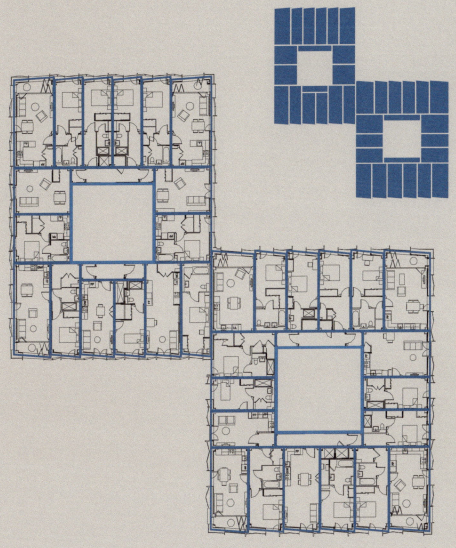

Fig 1 (facing)
Line drawing of George Street

Fig 2
Floor plan and modular layout

Fig 3
A view from Dingwall Road of the towers under construction

Fig 4
Visualisation showing potential future developments around the building

was required. The design draws heavily on the site history and the surrounding area's rich heritage of mid-century buildings including the iconic No.1 Croydon (commonly referred to as the '50p building'). Tide Construction were the developer and contractor with their sister company Vision Modular Systems providing the modular construction. The combination of this integrated business model and the pursuit of innovation delivery made development viable on a site that had been vacant for nearly 20 years and had been the subject of a number of previous applications. Realising a building of this scale and quality in 28 months required innovation in every aspect of design and construction from the extensive use of virtual reality and 3D printing for rapid prototyping at planning through to the angled modular facade and large format glazed terracotta diamonds which respond to orientation and aspect to create the distinctive architecture.

The development creates a new public realm for Croydon at ground level, a 'woodland winter garden' opening up a new green space on George Street and establishing a connection to the emerging cultural quarter. The ground floor incorporates a new art gallery space, a café and some flexible spaces which can incorporate a range of possible uses including business incubator spaces and artists' studio spaces. Residents of the building arrive via a grand double height entrance hall which opens up to a terrace and mezzanine spaces. This varied programme of different uses is unified by a 'giant order' 7.5m high GRC colonnade which runs around the base of the building. This colonnade is given a human scale with a combination of intricate etching, faceted forms and pressed glazed terracotta diamonds. The winter garden is covered by a glazed pyramid grid shell roof structure which spans over 20m to enclose the sheltered arrival square.

At the top of the towers the residents can enjoy spectacular views from a range of shared facilities including a gym, yoga room, games room, residents' lounge, screening room and entertaining room with show kitchen. Other facilities within the building include full concierge services, co-working facilities including meeting spaces and even a dog wash room. The tops of both towers enjoy access to roof terraces with the taller terrace providing a panoramic walkway offering 360-degree views across London.

Fig 5
Visualisation of the main entrance at ground floor level showing the public space in front of the building

Fig 6
Visualisation of the lower floors showing the public realm and active street frontage

Fig 7
Visualisation of the ground floor as it will be seen from East Croydon station

The towers provide a range of homes from studios to one-, two- and three-bedroom homes. Of these homes, 50% are dual-aspect and the remainder face east, south or west to ensure every home has direct sunlight. In the development 20% of homes are provided at reduced rent managed by the operator and this is made up of a mix of London Living Rent and 20% discount from market rate.

The proximity of East Croydon's transport hub provides the highest levels of connectivity by public transport with London Bridge and Gatwick both only 15 minutes away. Making the most of this connectivity to enhance Croydon's town centre is a crucial contribution in the decision to enable the 'super-density' of development in the area at around 2500 homes per hectare.

ADDING VALUE THROUGH DESIGN

This was the seventh modular development designed by HTA for Tide. This commitment to working together facilitates a process of continual improvement from project to project. An example of this at George Street was taking the structural technology established at the preceding project (Apex House) and evolving it to allow for a building which was 50% taller. This involved working closely with the same engineering team of MJH Structural Engineers and Barrett Mahony from the earliest concept design stages.

The collaborative nature of the project team extended to the approach to planning. An intensive sequence of pre-application meetings with the London Borough of Croydon created a dialogue that resulted in a significant increase in height from the existing planning consent on the site. To gain the confidence of officers a range of commitments were made to ensure quality, including the provision of three one-to-one bay mock-ups provided as part of the condition discharge process. Regular meetings with officers continued throughout the rapid construction programme ensuring that the original vision the team shared for the building was delivered.

Fig 8
Visualisation of the roofscape showing the scalloped roofline of the two towers

CASE STUDY 8: GEORGE STREET, CROYDON, LONDON

Fig 9
3D printed models showing the steel frame, the facade and the structural cores

Fig 10
The facade panels and aluminium support system

Another key aspect of the planning dialogue was the height of the towers balancing what was technically possible against their impact on townscape and microclimate. Particularly important was the height differential of the two towers and the consequences this had for wind loading, with differences of greater than six to eight storeys creating a structure that would have become unviable. Working through a range of views, wind tunnel testing and daylight assessments in parallel with the structural calculations allowed a structural solution to be finalised as part of the planning process and as a result, the two intersecting towers are joined structurally. Each tower has a central core which was slipformed and the modules assembled around them. A particular concern was that the cores would have a tendency to sway under heavy wind loads and this would act to pull apart the lower modular levels during construction. To counteract this the cores were tied together in three locations up through the building. The lifting beam for the modules was redesigned so that the modules near and under the ties could be suspended from the crane off centre to be manoeuvred into place. Finally, the sequencing of the module loading was strictly ordered in for the first 10 floors, always starting with the lower tower.

Given the proposal's unprecedented height as a modular building there was little data to demonstrate what if any stiffness the modules could contribute to the lateral stability of the building. Consequently, the structural engineers allowed for a slosh tank on top of tower A. Tide engaged the engineering department at Trinity College Dublin to undertake laser monitoring to evaluate the real world performance of building once all the modules were in place. This investigation has confirmed that the structure is much stiffer than expected and the slosh tank was subsequently omitted.

GETTING OUT OF THE GROUND

The project team's focus on developing a fully deliverable design at planning stage was evident by an immediate start on site upon receipt of planning consent and a programme of design activities concurrent with the construction programme.

During enabling works site investigation revealed that there were existing in-ground services close to and in places crossing the ownership boundary and some significant electrical and gas infrastructure actually traversing the site. As the design required an extensive two-storey basement to incorporate servicing it was necessary for the design team to redesign the perimeter of the basement to avoid existing services and phase the construction of the basement so that permits could be organised to divert services around the site to be able to disconnect and remove cabling running across it.

In February 2018 construction started with the first phase of work being the traditional concrete work up to the podium linking the two towers at first floor. This slab forms the base for installing the modules and given the height of the building this was required to be 2m thick. The twin cores were completed in December 2018 before the first module installation. The modules were stacked, fixed back to the core and sealed together using special cranes mounted on the top of the cores. The construction process operates floor-by-floor with each level being fire separated from the next. Prefabricated steel truss modules form a transfer structure under the top amenity floors to facilitate open-plan wide-span spaces for flexible use.

MODULAR INSTALLATION AND CRANAGE

The buildings incorporate over 1500 modules manufactured and installed by Vision Modular Systems from their purpose-built manufacturing facility in Bedford. The aim was to ensure all rooms were each fully enclosed within a module to avoid open-sided modules. The majority of internal fit-out to each room is installed in the factory including electrics and plumbing, kitchens and bathrooms, before the module is transported to the site. The team averaged 50 module installations a week and the installation completed in October 2019. Each module has a unique structural design for its location within the building, allowing for a highly efficient structure with the steel frame tapering in size from 300mm square sections at the base of the tower to 150mm sections at the top on a floor-by-floor basis. This efficiency results in a 6% gross to net gain compared to traditional construction and a floor-to-floor height which is around 200mm less than traditional construction. It also makes the most efficient use of materials.

The modular system incorporates a concrete floor, which aids fire and noise separation between apartments and also delivers a reassuring solidity, but as a result modules can be as heavy as 30t. At 44 storeys it was not possible to use a free-standing tower crane capable of lifting the module weights the distances required, so an elaborate sequence of crane erection was devised by the design team. Initially a self-erecting crane was installed tied to one of the cores. This then installed cranes onto each core and was then dis-erected and removed for the duration of the job. Towards the latter part of the project the taller core crane removed the lower core crane and the self-erecting tower crane returned to remove the taller core crane. With modules now in place the ties to secure the tower crane to the building had to

Fig 11 (top left)
The slipformed cores with the main cranes in position

Fig 12 (bottom left)
The towers under construction at the halfway point showing the bracing support between the cores

Fig 13 (right)
The towers under construction

Fig 14
A Vision Modular System module being craned into position

Fig 15
The towers under construction, showing the mast climbers working at two levels on the facade while modules are being installed

Fig 16
The towers under construction showing the mast climbers at work

be connected to the modules which were engineered to transmit the load horizontally to the core. All facade works to this face of the building had to be completed and the mast climbers had to be removed in time for this to take place. Cladding locally at the tie points was then completed using the permanent facade access system.

The cladding went up simultaneously with the modules, with installation of the glazed terracotta rainscreen cladding starting roughly 10 weeks after the module installations began. The speed of cladding installation was accelerated by pre-installing the support brackets on the modules in the factory. The cladding was completed two months after the final level of modules were installed.

The jewel-like cladding uses three different forms of glazed terracotta across the building and it was selected as the primary cladding material due to its combination of performance, appearance and durability. HTA worked closely with the specialist subcontractor (Century Facades) and manufacturer of the terracotta (NBK) to develop a glaze that echoed the marble of Fairfield Hall. A particular innovation was the large format glazed terracotta tiles used on the tower that fronts George Street. We understand that this was the first use of terracotta mounted onto an aluminium cassette system and this had a number of advantages, allowing the three-dimensional diamond shapes while producing a lighter weight panel that

CASE STUDY 8: GEORGE STREET, CROYDON, LONDON

Fig 17
The detail of the cladding showing the glazed finish to the terracotta

allowed rapid and accurate installation from the mast climbers. The high reflectance and angular planes that resulted from these diamonds combined with the facetted front face of the modules are a response to the particular challenge of the main elevation facing north on to George Street. This ensures that reflections animate the facade throughout the day despite its orientation.

The extruded terracotta tiles used for the taller tower element to the south are designed with varying saw-toothed profiles that create pools of glaze which exaggerate variations in colour. The plan form is facetted as well and the detail of the saw-tooth profiles vary with orientation to exaggerate each change in plane. In contrast to the lower tower the taller tower is organised into double height bays which create a calmer appearance, emphasising the tower's proportions.

Fig 18
The jewel-like cladding panels in place on the facade

Fig 19
A view of the facade nearing completion

The cladding in both facades is complemented by Juliet balconies with balustrades of perforated metal panels each folded to geometries that match the adjacent terracotta panels. In both towers the terracotta panel and metal framing components were modulated on each facade to respond to orientation and views from within the apartments. The angled facade panels create large window reveals to protect privacy on the inner faces while on other elevations they minimise window reveals to maximise light into the flats. The metal frame around each bay changes with orientation and overhangs to provide shading to the southerly facades while it is minimised to the northerly facades to maximise daylight.

HTA's overall composition concept was to create two towers that are related but subtly different, through proportion, material and pattern. This gives each part its own identity and avoids the mass merging into one, particularly when viewed from a distance.

CASE STUDY 8: GEORGE STREET, CROYDON, LONDON

Fig 20
The towers with all modules installed

Fig 21
The cladding to the entrance under construction

The build-to-rent development was forward-funded by Greystar and Henderson Park and will be operated by the former. As volumetric modular construction such as this can allow rental returns in around half the time of traditional construction it is likely to play a central role in the future of build-to-rent – Greystar have seen the advantage of becoming an early adopter.

The continuity of the team, driving a culture of innovation and a focus on delivering built outcomes, enabled the entire project to be delivered from first concept sketch to handover in just 39 months. It is a case study in the potential of modular construction to contribute to solving the UK's housing crisis while delivering buildings of the highest architectural quality and with world-leading engineering.

Fig 22
Interior of open plan living space

Fig 23
The building nearing completion showing the reflectivity of the facade

FACTS

Location	George Street, Croydon London, CR0 1LF
Planning authority	London Borough of Croydon
Client	Tide Construction Ltd
Main contractor and developer	Tide Construction Ltd
Modular manufacturer	Vision Modular Systems
Module construction	Steel-framed with concrete floor
Architect	HTA Design LLP
Type of housing	546 build-to-rent units
Start date	January 2018
Completion date	August 2020
Construction period	31 months
Number of homes	546 homes
Number of modules	c. 1500 modules
Number of storeys	38 and 44
Site area	0.22ha
Operator	Greystar

CASE STUDY 8: GEORGE STREET, CROYDON, LONDON

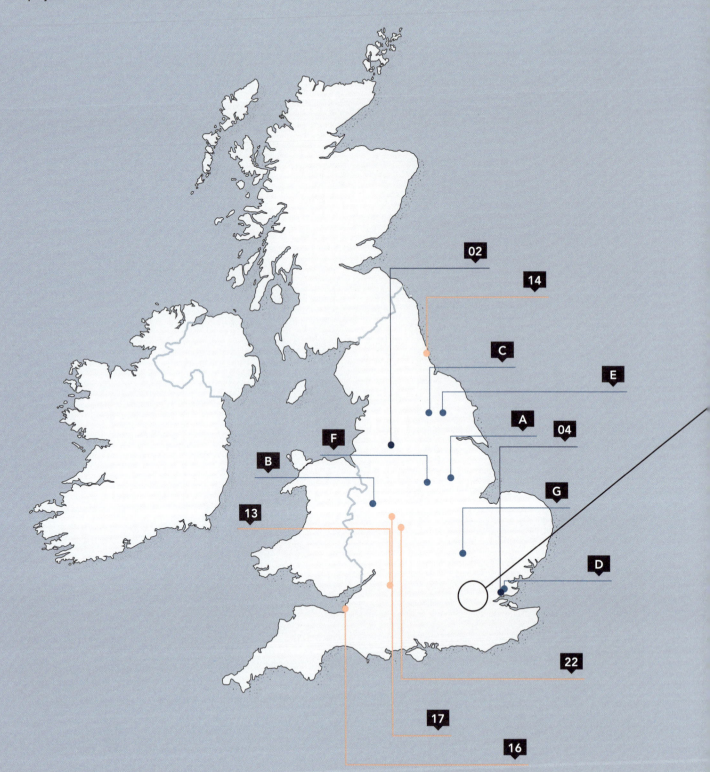

Project Map

Showing the locations of both the projects and factories from in this book

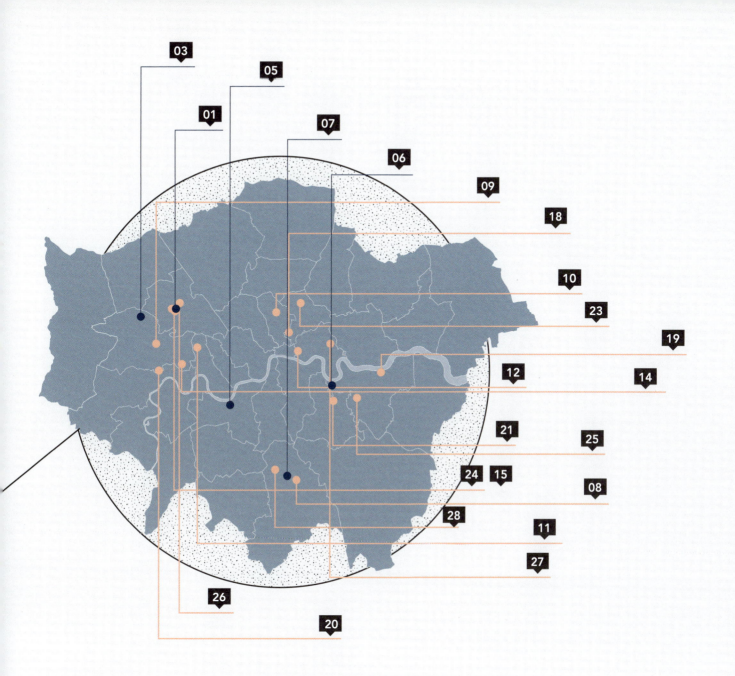

REFERENCES

CHAPTER 1: TOWARDS A MODULAR ARCHITECTURE

1. Rachel Cooper, 'Home ownership falls for first time in a century', *The Telegraph*, https://www.telegraph.co.uk/finance/property/house-prices/10005586/Home-ownership-falls-for-first-time-in-a-century.html, 2013, (accessed 7 May 2019).
2. Clive Turner, NHBC Foundation and Richards Partington Architects, 'Homes through the decades', *NHBC*, http://www.nhbc.co.uk/cms/publish/consumer/NewsandComment/HomesThroughTheDecades.pdf, 2015, (accessed 4 June 2019).
3. Central Housing Advisory Committee, *Living in Flats: Report of the Flats Sub-committee*, H.M. Stationery Office, 1952 citied in Stefan Muthesius, Miles Glendinning and Nicholas Warr, *Towers for the Welfare State: An Architectural History of British Multi-storey Housing 1945–1970*, University of Edinburgh, 2017, p 10.
4. HMSO, Housing, White Paper, 1963.
5. Laing Construction, 'Promo video', *YouTube*, https://www.youtube.com/watch?v=CgwFXujj52M, 2017 (accessed 18 July 2019).
6. Sir Michael Latham, 'Constructing the Team', *Constructing Excellence*, http://constructingexcellence.org.uk/wp-content/uploads/2014/10/Constructing-the-team-The-Latham-Report.pdf, 1994, (accessed 3 April 2019).
7. Construction Task Force, 'Rethinking Construction', *Constructing Excellence*, http://constructingexcellence.org.uk/wp-content/uploads/2014/10/rethinking_construction_report.pdf, 1998 (accessed 5 April 2019).
8. Mark Farmer, 'The Farmer Review of the UK Construction Labour Model', *Construction Leadership Council*, http://www.constructionleadershipcouncil.co.uk/wp-content/uploads/2016/10/Farmer-Review.pdf, 2016, (accessed 22 August 2018).
9. Ibid.
10. MHCLG, 'Fixing our broken housing market', *GOV*, https://www.gov.uk/government/publications/fixing-our-broken-housing-market, 2017, (accessed 24 October 2018).
11. MHCLG, 'Independent Review of Building Regulations and Fire Safety: Final Report', *GOV*, https://www.gov.uk/government/publications/independent-review-of-building-regulations-and-fire-safety-final-report, 2018, (accessed 7 February 2019).
12. Raynsford Review Task Force, 'Planning 2020 – Raynsford Review of Planning in England', *TCPA*, https://www.tcpa.org.uk/raynsford-review, 2018, (accessed 7 January 2019).
13. Housing Design Awards, *Archive*, https://hdawards.org/archive/, (accessed 20 March 2019).

CHAPTER 2: A MODERN MODULAR VERNACULAR

1. UCL, 'New housing design in England overwhelmingly "mediocre" or "poor"', *UCL News*, https://www.ucl.ac.uk/news/2020/jan/new-housing-design-england-overwhelmingly-mediocre-or-poor, 21 January 2020 (accessed 21 January 2020).
2. MHCLG, 'Government champions innovation in bid to build well-designed homes', *GOV*, https://www.gov.uk/government/news/government-champions-innovation-in-bid-to-build-well-designed-homes, 2018 (accessed 8 June 2019).
3. Building Better, 'Building Beautiful Commission', *GOV*, https://www.gov.uk/government/groups/building-better-building-beautiful-commission, 2019, (accessed 3 October 2019).
4. The Housing Forum, 'Building Homes Better – the quality challenge', *Housing Forum*, http://www.housingforum.org.uk/resources/building-homes-better---the-quality-challenge, 2017, (accessed 30 June 2019).
5. APPG, 'APPG for Excellence in the Built Environment: More homes, fewer complaints', *CIOB*, https://policy.ciob.org/resources/appg-excellence-built-environment-homes-fewer-complaints/, 2016, (accessed 22 April 2019).

6   Homes England, 'Boost for housing market as Japan's biggest housebuilder – Sekisui House – moves into UK', *GOV*, https://www.gov.uk/government/news/boost-for-housing-market-as-japans-biggest-housebuilder-sekisui-house-moves-into-uk, 2019, (Accessed 4 November 2019).

7   Matt Weaver and Martin Wainwright, 'Pioneering flats "could blow down"', *The Guardian*, https://www.theguardian.com/society/2005/nov/01/communities.politics, 2005, (accessed 15 May 2018).

8   'Independent timber trends report highlights significant growth potential in housing sector for structural timber frame', *Structural Timber*,https://www.structuraltimber.co.uk/news/structural-timber-news/independent-timber-trends-report-highlights-significant-growth-potential-in-housing-sector-for-structural-timber-fram/, n.d., (accessed 1 July 2019).

9   William Johnson, 'Lessons from Japan: A comparative study of the market drivers for prefabrication in Japanese and UK private housing development', *Masters thesis – London: University College London*, https://discovery.ucl.ac.uk/id/eprint/5082/1/5082.pdf, 2007, (accessed 12 July 2019).

10 James Wilmore, 'How Ilke and Places for People aim to make modular mainstream', *Inside Housing*, https://www.insidehousing.co.uk/insight/insight/how-ilke-and-places-for-people-aim-to-make-modular-mainstream-61994, 2019, (Accessed 14 September 2019).

11 Hamish Champ, 'Goldman Sachs sinks £75m into modular homes firm', *Building*, https://www.building.co.uk/news/goldman-sachs-sinks-75m-into-modular-homes-firm/5098973.article, 2019, (Accessed 14 April 2019).

12 William Johnson, 'Lessons from Japan: A comparative study of the market drivers for prefabrication in Japanese and UK private housing development', *Masters thesis – London: University College London*, https://discovery.ucl.ac.uk/id/eprint/5082/1/5082.pdf, 2007, (accessed 12 July 2019).

13 HTA Design LLP, 'HTA Potton House', *Configurator Creatomus*, https://configurator.creatomus.com/project/hta, (accessed 5 September 2018).

CHAPTER 3: MAKING A MODULAR METROPOLIS

1   'Living with Beauty', The report of the Building Better, Building Beautiful Commission, https://assets.publishing.service.gov.uk/government/uploads/system/uploads/attachment_data/file/861832/Living_with_beauty_BBBBC_report.pdf, 2020, (accessed 10th February)

2   Daniela Krug and Professor John Miles, 'Offsite Construction', *Build Offsite*, https://www.buildoffsite.com/content/uploads/2015/03/BoS_offsiteconstruction_1307091.pdf, 2013, (accessed 17 November 2018).

3   Daniela Krug and Professor John Miles, 'Offsite Construction', *Build Offsite*, https://www.buildoffsite.com/content/uploads/2015/03/BoS_offsiteconstruction_1307091.pdf, 2013, (accessed 17 November 2018).

4   Daniela Krug and Professor John Miles, 'Offsite Construction', *Build Offsite*, https://www.buildoffsite.com/content/uploads/2015/03/BoS_offsiteconstruction_1307091.pdf, 2013, (accessed 17 November 2018).

5   'UK House Price Index', *Land Registry*, https://landregistry.data.gov.uk/app/ukhpi, 2019, (accessed 2 January 2020).

6   ONS, 'Construction statistics', Great Britain: 2018, *ONS Construction Industry*, https://www.ons.gov.uk/businessindustryandtrade/constructionindustry/articles/constructionstatistics/2018#output-price-indices, 2018, (accessed 14 July 2019).

7   Mark Farmer, 'The Farmer Review of the UK Construction Labour Model', *Construction Leadership Council*, http://www.constructionleadershipcouncil.co.uk/wp-content/uploads/2016/10/Farmer-Review.pdf, 2016, (accessed 22 August 2018).

8   Experian Business Strategies and SAMI Consulting Limited, '2020 Vision – The Future of UK Construction', *citb – Construction Skills*, https://www.citb.co.uk/documents/research/csn%20outputs/2020-vision-future-uk-construction.pdf (accessed 2 January 2020).

9   Faisal Alazzaz and Andrew Whyte, 'Uptake of Off-site Construction: Benefit and Future Application', *World Academy of Science, Engineering and Technology International Journal of Civil and Environmental Engineering*, Vol. 8, Issue 12, 2014, https://pdfs.semanticscholar.org/1c97/2a50a960192a759b121f088b7f5c2a3f35d8.pdf?_ga=2.12037748.191698386.1579691991-1902665941.1579691991, (accessed on 29 August 2019).

CHAPTER 4: ARCHITECTS AS DESIGNERS IN INDUSTRY

1. *Phaidon*, 'Why Louis Kahn would often talk to bricks', *Phaidon*, https://uk.phaidon.com/agenda/architecture/articles/2019/january/16/why-louis-kahn-would-often-talk-to-bricks/, 2019, (accessed 13 December 2019).
2. Atli Magnus, 'The Construction Kit and the Assembly Line – Walter Gropius' Concepts for Rationalizing Architecture', *Arts 2018*, https://doi.org/10.3390/arts7040095, 2018, (accessed 13 February 2019).
3. Henry Ford and Samuel Crowther, *My Life and Work*, Garden City, 1922, p 72.
4. Alex Gkikas and Dr Gillian Menzies, 'Greenford Green Block 5', *Heriot Watt*, https://www.hta.co.uk/publications, 2017 (accessed 20 January 2020).
5. Daniela Krug and Professor John Miles, 'Offsite Construction', *Build Offsite*, https://www.buildoffsite.com/content/uploads/2015/03/BoS_offsiteconstruction_1307091.pdf, 2013, (accessed 17 November 2018).
6. Daniela Krug and Professor John Miles, 'Offsite Construction', *Build Offsite*, https://www.buildoffsite.com/content/uploads/2015/03/BoS_offsiteconstruction_1307091.pdf, 2013, (accessed 17 November 2018).
7. Mark Farmer, 'The Farmer Review of the UK Construction Labour Model', Construction Leadership Council, http://www.constructionleadershipcouncil.co.uk/wp-content/uploads/2016/10/Farmer-Review.pdf, 2016, (accessed 22 August 2018).
8. Berkeley Modular, *Berkeley Group*, https://www.berkeleygroup.co.uk/about-us/our-brands/berkeley-modular (accessed 6 October 2019).
9. Dr Gemma Burgess, 'Housing Digital Built Britain Network', *Cambridge Centre for Housing & Planning Research*, https://www.cchpr.landecon.cam.ac.uk/Research/Start-Year/2018/digital_built_britain_housing_network/housing_network_final_report/housing_network_final_report/at_download/file, 2018, (accessed 21 September 2019).

CHAPTER 5: MAKING SURE IT STACKS UP

1. Joey Gardiner, 'Mark Farmer to be named government MMC champion', *Building*, https://www.building.co.uk/news/mark-farmer-to-be-named-government-mmc-champion/5102521.article, 2019, (accessed 9 February 2020).
2. Mark Lawson, Ray Ogden and Chris Goodier, 'Construction issues for concrete modules' in *Design in Modular Construction*, CRC Press, 2014, p 220.
3. 'Modern Methods of Construction: introducing the MMC definition framework', *Modern Methods of Construction Working Group MHCLG*, http://www.cast-consultancy.com/wp-content/uploads/2019/03/MMC-I-Pad-base_GOVUK-FINAL_SECURE.pdf, 2019, (accessed 8 August 2019).
4. Prism app, https://www.prism-app.io/, (accessed 6 November 2019).

CHAPTER 6: THE MODULAR WORLD

1. MHCLG, 'Leeds gets building as construction corridor continues to forge path across North of England', *GOV*, https://www.gov.uk/government/news/leeds-gets-building-as-construction-corridor-continues-to-forge-path-across-north-of-england, 2020, (accessed 13 January 2020).
2. Nick Bertram, Steffen Fuchs, Jan Mischke, Robert Palter, Gernot Strube and Jonathan Woetzel, 'Modular Construction: From projects to products', *McKinsey & Company*, https://www.mckinsey.com/~/media/mckinsey/industries/capital%20projects%20and%20infrastructure/our%20insights/modular%20construction%20from%20projects%20to%20products%20new/modular-construction-from-projects-to-products-full-report-new.ashx, 2019, (accessed 25 November 2019).
3. Mark Farmer, 'The Farmer Review of the UK Construction Labour Model', *Construction Leadership Council*, http://www.constructionleadershipcouncil.co.uk/wp-content/uploads/2016/10/Farmer-Review.pdf, 2016, (accessed 22 August 2018).
4. Tino Chang, 'China to promote prefabricated construction', *Turner & Townsend*, https://www.turnerandtownsend.com/en/perspectives/china-to-promote-prefabricated-construction-international-construction-market-survey-2018/, 2018, (accessed 7 October 2018).
5. Tino Chang, 'China to promote prefabricated construction', *Turner & Townsend*, https://www.turnerandtownsend.com/en/perspectives/china-to-promote-prefabricated-construction-international-construction-market-survey-2018/, 2018, (accessed 7 October 2018).

REFERENCES

6   *The Economist*, 'The turmoil in Hong Kong stems in part from its unaffordable housing', *The Economist*, https://www.economist.com/china/2019/08/22/the-turmoil-in-hong-kong-stems-in-part-from-its-unaffordable-housing, 2019, (accessed 3 October 2019).

7   Orla Dwyer, 'A new record high: The average monthly rent in Ireland is now over €1,400', *TheJournal.ie*, https://www.thejournal.ie/daft-latest-rental-report-2019-4886754-Nov2019/, 2019, (accessed 5 December 2019).

8   'Social, Economic and Land Use Study of the Impact of PBSA in Dublin City', *EY consultants, Coyne Research and Dublin City Council*, <https://assets.ey.com/content/dam/ey-sites/ey-com/en_ie/topics/transaction-advisory-services/ey-how-does-putting-purpose-at-the-centre-transform-programme-delivery.pdf>, 2018, (accessed 7 November 2019).

9   ONS, 'Housing affordability in England and Wales: 2018', *ONS.GOV*, https://www.ons.gov.uk/peoplepopulationandcommunity/housing/bulletins/housingaffordabilityinenglandandwales/2018, 2019, (accessed 17 May 2019).

CHAPTER 7: BUILDING A MORE MODULAR FUTURE

1   Homes England, 'About us', *GOV*, https://www.gov.uk/government/organisations/homes-england/about, n.d., (accessed 10 February 2020).

CASE STUDY 1: APEX HOUSE

1   NLA research, 'Factory Made Housing – A solution for London?', *NLA*, p 70, http://legacy.newlondonarchitecture.org/docs/factory-made_housing_nla_reseach.pdf, 2018, (accessed 8 September 2019).

CASE STUDY 2: NEW ISLINGTON

1   Comment from Urban Splash 25th birthday by founder Tom Bloxham.

CASE STUDY 3: GREENFORD QUAY

1   NLA research, 'Factory Made Housing – A solution for London?', *NLA*, p 116, http://legacy.newlondonarchitecture.org/docs/factory-made_housing_nla_reseach.pdf, 2018, (accessed 6 August 2019).

CASE STUDY 5: MAPLETON CRESCENT

1   Mapleton Crescent, Wandsworth has received and been shortlisted for several awards. https://metwork.co.uk/work/mapleton-crescent/.

2   Rowan Moore, 'Mapleton Crescent: the London high-rise factory-built in Bedfordshire', *The Observer*, 20 May 2018.

3   Pocket Living have commissioned LSE to undertake research into the preferences of Pocket customers to refine their offer within future programmes of development.

4   At 476sqm or 0.05ha the site constitutes a small site under the Mayor of London's New London Plan (below 0.25ha).

5   www.pocketliving.com.

6   Based on tender prices proposing concrete framing.

7   BBC London, 'Could Londoners soon be living in "modular" homes?', https://www.youtube.com/watch?v=hxt9Ha7ORpY, 28 February 2019. Caroline Davies reports.

8   Rowan Moore. (2018) 'Mapleton Crescent: the London high-rise factory-built in Bedfordshire', *The Observer*, 20 May 2018.

CASE STUDY 6: UNION WHARF

1   Department for Communities and Local Government, 'Fixing our broken housing market', *GOV*, https://assets.publishing.service.gov.uk/government/uploads/system/uploads/attachment_data/file/590464/Fixing_our_broken_housing_market_-_print_ready_version.pdf, February 2017, (accessed 14 February 2020).

FURTHER READING

Aitchison, Mathew et al., *Prefab Housing and the Future of Building: Product to Process*, London, Lund Humphries Publishers Ltd, 2018.

Distinctively Local, HTA Design, Pollard Thomas Edwards (PTE), PRP and Proctor & Matthews Architects, www.distinctively-local.co.uk, (accessed 17 February 2020).

Dorries, Cornelia and Sarah Zahradnik, *Construction and Design Manual: Container and Modular Buildings*, Berlin, DOM Publishers, 2016.

Groak, Stephen, *The Idea of Building: Thought and Action in the Design and Production of Buildings*, Abingdon, Routledge, 1992.

Knaack, Ulrich, Sharon Chung-Klatte and Reinhard Hasselbach, *Prefabricated Systems: Principles of Construction*, Basel, Switzerland, Birkhäuser, 2010.

Lawson, Dr Mark, Ray Ogden and Chris Goodlier, *Design in Modular Construction*, Boca Raton, FL, CRC Press, 2014.

Modular Systems, *DETAIL Magazine*, Serie, 2001. 4.

Murray-Parkes, James, Yu Bai, George Konstandakos, John Lucchetti, Brendon McNiven and Ben Forbes, *Model Code for the Design of Modular Structures*, Clayton, Australia, Monash University, 2016.

Muthesius, Stefan, Miles Glendinning and Nicholas Warr, *Towers for the Welfare State: an Architectural History of British Multi-Storey Housing 1945-1970*, Edinburgh, University of Edinburgh, 2017.

Smith, Ryan E. and John D. Quale (eds.), *Offsite Architecture, Constructing the Future*, Abingdon, Routledge, 2017.

Stephenson, Greg, *Places for the People: Prefabs in Post-War Britain*, London, Batsford Ltd, 2003.

Winchester, Simon, *Exactly: How Precision Engineers Changed the Modern World*, Glasgow, Williams Collins, 2018.

Woudhuysen, James and Ian Abley, *Why is Construction so Backward?*, Hoboken, NJ, Wiley and Sons, 2004.

INDEX

Page numbers in bold indicate figures.

461 Dean Street, Brooklyn, New York 52, 136, 137, **138**

A
AD+RG 123-124
Addiscombe Grove, Croydon, London 55, 90, **91**
ADDP Architects LLP *see* Clement Canopy, Singapore
Allerton Bywater, Leeds **15**
Allford Hall Monaghan Morris (AHMM)
    Officers' House, Woolwich 128, **129**
    Raines Court, Hackney 14, 52, 53-54, **53**, **54**
Alton Estate, Wandsworth, London **9**
apartment modularisation 58-60, **59**, **60**, **61**, 88
Apex Airspace 64, **64**
Apex House, Wembley, London 133, **146**, 147-155, **147**, **148**, **150**, **152**, **153**, **154**, **155**
Assael *see* Union Wharf, Greenwich, London
Australia **116**, 119, **119**, 120
Aylesbury Estate, Southwark, London 10, **10**

B
Balders Have, Denmark **122**
Barratt Homes **15**, 16-17, **17**, 32
Beechwood West, Basildon, Essex **42**, 89, **89**, **174**, 175-181, **175**, **176**, **177**, **178**, **179**, **180**
Berkeley Homes/Berkeley Modular 46, **47**, 55, 126, 128, **129**
Bo Klok 132
Bollo Lane, Ealing, London 66, **67**
Building Information Modelling (BIM) 32, **89**, 93

C
C+W O'Brien Architects **125**
Caledonian Modular 46, **47**, 52, 55, 133
Carbon Challenge 14
Carbon Dynamic 81-82, **82**
Cartwright Pickard 12-13, **13**, 14
Chapter Highbury II, Islington, London 62, 114, **115**
Chapter White City, Shepherd's Bush, London 22-23, **22**, **23**, 76
Chase Farm, Nottinghamshire **42**, 86
China 121
CIMC 55, 119, 121, 122
citizenM Hotel, Tower Hill, London 65, 109-110, **109**, **110**, 131
citizenM New York Bowery Hotel, New York **134**, **135**, 136

Clarke, George 39, **40**, 96
Clement Canopy, Singapore **73**, 74, 131, **198**, 199-203, **199**, **200**, **203**
climate emergency 18, 25, 92
College Road, Croydon, London **140**
Concrete Architectural Associates **134**, **135**
construction cost savings 99-103, **102**, **103**, 106-108, **106**, **107**, 111-113, **111**
construction process 65
    see also factory production; installation
contracting *see* procurement
cost savings 99-103, **102**, **103**, 106-108, **106**, **107**, 111-113, **111**
council housing 7, 9-11, **10**, 20-21, 32
cross-laminated timber (CLT) 36, 41, **60**, 92, 103, 162
    Dyson Village, Malmesbury, Wiltshire 81-82, **82**
    PLACE/Ladywell, Lewisham 33-34, **33**
    Watts Grove, Tower Hamlets 70, **71**
    Y:Cube, Mitcham 104, **105**
    see also Beechwood West, Basildon, Essex; New Islington, Manchester
customisation 43-44, 48, **48**, 88-89, **89**

D
De Meeuw 130
debt reduction 106-107, **107**
Denmark 121, **122**
design 25-27
    see also modularisation
design for manufacture and assembly (DfMA) approach 43, 85-88, 96-97, 118
Design for Manufacture competition 14, **15**
DMD Modular 131
Dragages Singapore Pte Ltd 131
    see also Clement Canopy, Singapore
Dymaxion House 80
Dyson Village, Malmesbury, Wiltshire 81-82, **82**

E
Eames, Charles 80, **80**
Eames, Ray 80, **80**
Egan Report 11, 12
Elements Europe 55, 133
    Addiscombe Grove, Croydon 55, 90, **91**
    Union Wharf, Greenwich 55, **73**, 133, **192**, 193-197, **193**, **194**, **197**
    Urban House Kidbrooke, Greenwich 46, **47**
embodied carbon 24-25, 92, 141
environmental impacts 18, 24-25, 68-69, **68**, 92, 141
Erskine, Ralph 11

Essential Living 74
    see also Union Wharf, Greenwich, London
Essmodular 126

F

Fab House, North Shields 39, **40**, **96**
facade options **61**
factory production 31-32, 43, 44, **65**, 73-74
    cost savings 101-103, **103**, 107-108
    health and safety 108
    social benefits 65
    sustainability benefits 68-69, **68**, 92
Fallingwater, Pennsylvania **79**
'Farmer Review of the UK Construction Labour Model' 18
FCH Architects **133**
Felda House, Wembley, London 94-95, **94**, **95**
Fleetwood 119
Forest City 136, 137, **138**
Forta PRO 55, 126, 128, **129**
Foster, Norman 80
Full Stack 136
Fuller, Buckminster 80

G

George Street, Croydon, London **26**, **27**, 55, **63**, 74, **75**, **98**, 133, **142**, **204**, 205-216, **205**, **206**, **207**, **208**, **209**, **211**, **212**, **213**, **214**, **215**, **216**, **217**
Glen Iris Residential Building, Australia **116**, 119, **119**
Glenn Howells Architects **161**
Greenford Quay, Ealing, London **2**, **20**, 58, **59**, **68**, **69**, 74, **164**, 165-173, **165**, **166**, **168**, **170**, **172**, **173**
Greenwich Millennium Village, London 11, **11**
Grenfell Tower, London 4, 18
Greystar 74, 137, 141, 205, 215
    see also Greenford Quay, Ealing, London
Grimshaw, Nicholas 80
Gropius, Walter 80
Guerdon Modular Buildings 136

H

Hanham Hall, Bristol 14, 16-17, **17**
health and safety 108, 118
Heartlands, Trevenson Park, Cornwall 44, 48, **48**
Hester Architects **133**
Hickory Group 119, 120
high-rise modular construction 62-64, **62**, **63**, 74, 75
Hinkley Point power station 55, 133
Hi-Tech movement 80
Home of the Future design **30**
home ownership trends 4, **5**
Homes England 31, 38, 132, 143, 145, 161-163
Hong Kong 74, 122, **122**, 123-124, 139
Hope Street, Liverpool 126, **133**

Hopkins, Michael 80
housing crisis 4
HTA Design LLP **25**, **64**, **88**
    Allerton Bywater, Leeds **15**
    Apex House, Wembley 133, **146**, 147-155, **147**, **148**, **150**, **152**, **153**, **154**, **155**
    Chapter Highbury II, Islington **62**, 114, **115**
    Chapter White City, Shepherd's Bush 22-23, **22**, **23**, **76**
    College Road, Croydon **140**
    Felda House, Wembley 94-95, **94**, **95**
    George Street, Croydon **26**, **27**, 55, **63**, 74, **75**, **98**, 133, **142**, **204**, 205-216, **205**, **206**, **207**, **208**, **209**, **211**, **212**, **213**, **214**, **215**, **216**, **217**
    Greenford Quay, Ealing **2**, **20**, 58, **59**, **68**, **69**, 74, **164**, 165-173, **165**, **166**, **168**, **170**, **172**, **173**
    Greenwich Millennium Village 11, **11**
    Hanham Hall, Bristol 14, 16-17, **17**
    Heartlands, Trevenson Park, Cornwall 44, 48, **48**
    Home of the Future design **30**
    The Hundred House design **31**, **42**
    Mill Way, Cambridgeshire **84**
    Shubette House, Wembley 52, 56-57, **57**
    Union Wharf, Greenwich 55, **73**, 133, **192**, 193-197, **193**, **194**, **197**
    Wong Chuk Hang Student Residence, Hong Kong 123-124
Huf Haus 32
The Hundred House design **31**, **42**

I

Igloo 44, 48
Ijburg, Amsterdam **45**
ilke Homes 41, **42**, **86**
IMAX Modular Pte Ltd 122
Innocel, Hong Kong 122, **122**
installation 60, **61**, **62**, **63**-64, **63**, **65**
Ireland 125-126
Irwell Riverside, Manchester **49**, 161, **161**

J

JaJa architects **122**
Japan 126, **127**

K

Kahn, Louis 78
Katerra 136
Keepmoat Homes 41, **42**, **86**
Kingspan TEK system 14, 16-17, **17**, 35

L

La Trobe Tower, Melbourne, Australia 119, 120
Latham Report 11
Latvia 126

INDEX

Le Corbusier 79, **79**
Leeghwaterstraat, Netherlands **130**
Legal & General Homes 21, 41
Leigh & Orange Architects **122**
Liberty Heights, Wolverhampton 52
light gauge steel (LGS) panels 36
Lindbäcks 132
local authorities 9-11, 20-21, 32, 87

M
Mansion House, Manchester **162**, 163
Mapleton Crescent, Wandsworth, London **50**, **182**, 183-191, **183**, **184**, **185**, **186**, **187**, **188**, **189**, **190**, **191**
Mecanoo **130**, 131
Metropolitan Workshop
 Addiscombe Grove, Croydon 55, 90, **91**
 Mapleton Crescent, Wandsworth **50**, **182**, 183-191, **183**, **184**, **185**, **186**, **187**, **188**, **189**, **190**, **191**
 Mill Way, Cambridgeshire **84**
Modern Methods of Construction (MMC) 31, 99-103, **100**, **102**, **103**, 106-108, **106**, **107**, 111-113, **111**
Modscape **116**, 119
modularisation
 apartments 58-60, **59**, **60**, **61**, **88**
 terraced housing 37, **37**
Murray Grove, Hackney, London 12-13, **13**, 14, 52

N
Nationally Described Space Standards (NDSS) 19, 37, 83
Netherlands 130-131, **130**
New Islington, Manchester **28**, 38, **156**, 157-163, **157**, **158**, **159**, **160**
New Zealand 130
Nordic Homes 126
Norway 130

O
Officers' House, Woolwich, London 128, **129**
ONV Architects **122**

P
Packaged House 80
Peabody Trust 14, 52
 Murray Grove, Hackney 12-13, **13**, 14, 52
 Raines Court, Hackney 14, 52, 53-54, **53**, **54**
PLACE/Ladywell, Lewisham, London 33-34, **33**
Pocket Living
 Addiscombe Grove, Croydon 55, 90, **91**
 Bollo Lane, Ealing 66, **67**
 Mapleton Crescent, Wandsworth **50**, **182**, 183-191, **183**, **184**, **185**, **186**, **187**, **188**, **189**, **190**, **191**
Poland 131

Polcom 55, 109-110, **109**, **110**, 131, 136
Pollard Thomas Edwards *see* Beechwood West, Basildon, Essex
Port Loop, Birmingham 161, **161**
Portakabin 38
precast concrete panels 36
prefabs, post-war 7-8, **8**, 36
pre-manufactured value (PMV) 103, **103**
Prescott, John 14
Prime Living, Dublin **125**, 126
procurement 4, 9, 11, 32, 43, 85, 87, 102, **102**, 134-136
Prouvé, Jean 79, **80**
PRP 66, **67**

R
RAD Urban 136
Raines Court, Hackney, London 14, 52, 53-54, **53**, **54**
Red Road Estate, Glasgow 10, **10**
rental trends 4, **5**
Rogers, Richard 80
Rogers Stirk Harbour + Partners 33-34, **33**, 104, **105**
Ronan Point, London 10
rooftop extensions 64, **64**
rothelowman 120

S
Scandi Byg 121
Sekisui House 31, 38, 126, **127**, 132, 163
self-build 32
shedkm 38
 Irwell Riverside, Manchester **49**, 161, **161**
 Mansion House, Manchester **162**, 163
 New Islington, Manchester **28**, 38, **156**, 157-163, **157**, **158**, **159**, **160**
Sheppard Robson 109-110, **109**, **110**
SHoP Architects 137, **138**
Shubette House, Wembley, London 52, 56-57, **57**
SIG Build Systems 33-34, **33**, 38, 104, **105**, 159
Singapore 74, 131, 139
 Clement Canopy **73**, 74, 131, **198**, 199-203, **199**, **200**, **203**
Skanska USA 137, **138**
Skystone 136
standardisation 6, 10, 19, 37, 43-44, 48, 83, 85
 see also modularisation
Stephen B. Jacobs Group **134**, **135**
Stoll Long Architects **116**
structural frames 35-36
structural insulated panels (SIPs) 35, 103, 112
sustainability benefits 68-69, **68**, 92, 141
Sustainer Homes 130
Swan NU Build 41, 89, 145
 Beechwood West, Basildon, Essex **42**, 89, **89**, **174**, 175-181, **175**, **176**, **177**, **178**, **179**, **180**
 Watts Grove, Tower Hamlets 70, **71**
Sweden 132

T

TDO Architecture 39, **40**, **96**
tendering 43, 85, 87, 102, **102**
terraced housing modularisation 37, **37**
Tide Construction **25**, 55
    Apex House, Wembley 133, **146**, 147-155, **147**, **148**, **150**, **152**, **153**, **154**, **155**
    Bollo Lane, Ealing 66, **67**
    Chapter Highbury II, Islington **62**, 114, **115**
    Chapter White City, Shepherd's Bush 22-23, **22**, **23**, **76**
    College Road, Croydon **140**
    Felda House, Wembley 94-95, **94**, **95**
    George Street, Croydon **26**, **27**, 55, **63**, 74, **75**, **98**, 133, **142**, **204**, 205-216, **205**, **206**, **207**, **208**, **209**, **211**, **212**, **213**, **214**, **215**, **216**, 217
    Greenford Quay, Ealing **2**, **20**, 58, **59**, 68, 69, 74, **164**, 165-173, **165**, **166**, **168**, **170**, **172**, 173
    Mapleton Crescent, Wandsworth **50**, **182**, 183-191, **183**, **184**, **185**, **186**, **187**, **188**, **189**, **190**, **191**
    Shubette House, Wembley 52, 56-57, **57**
timber frames 35
TopHat 41, 132, 133
Trivselhus 132

U

Union Wharf, Greenwich, London 55, **73**, 133, **192**, 193-197, **193**, **194**, **197**
Unité d'Habitation, Marseille, France 79, **79**
United States 131, 134-136, **134**, **135**
    461 Dean Street, Brooklyn, New York 52, 136, 137, **138**
    Urban House Kidbrooke, Greenwich, London 46, **47**
Urban Splash/Urban Splash Modular 31, 38, 132, 133, 142, 145
    Fab House, North Shields 39, **40**, **96**
    Irwell Riverside, Manchester **49**, 161, **161**
    Mansion House, Manchester **162**, 163
    New Islington, Manchester **28**, 38, **156**, 157-163, **157**, **158**, **159**, **160**
    Port Loop, Birmingham 161, **161**
Ursem 130-131

V

vertical stacking **61**
Vision Modular Systems **24**, **25**, 52, 55, 133, **142**
    Apex House, Wembley 133, **146**, 147-155, **147**, **148**, **150**, **152**, **153**, **154**, **155**
    Bollo Lane, Ealing 66, **67**
    Chapter Highbury II, Islington **62**, 114, **115**
    Chapter White City, Shepherd's Bush 22-23, **22**, **23**, **76**
    College Road, Croydon **140**
    Felda House, Wembley 94-95, **94**, **95**
    George Street, Croydon **26**, **27**, 55, **63**, 74, **75**, **98**, 133, **142**, **204**, 205-216, **205**, **206**, **207**, **208**, **209**, **211**, **212**, **213**, **214**, **215**, **216**, 217
    Greenford Quay, Ealing **2**, **20**, 58, **59**, 68, 69, 74, **164**, 165-173, **165**, **166**, **168**, **170**, **172**, 173
    Mapleton Crescent, Wandsworth **50**, **182**, 183-191, **183**, **184**, **185**, **186**, **187**, **188**, **189**, **190**, **191**
    Shubette House, Wembley 52, 56-57, **57**

W

Wachsmann, Konrad 80
Watts Grove, Tower Hamlets, London 70, **71**
Waugh Thistleton 70, **71**
WilkinsonEyre 81-82, **82**
Wong Chuk Hang Student Residence, Hong Kong 122, 123-124
Wright, Frank Lloyd 78, **79**

Y

Y:Cube, Mitcham, London 104, **105**

Z

zero carbon housing 14, 16-17, **17**

IMAGE CREDITS

Author headshots
Tom Campbell

Preface
Fig 1 – HTA Design LLP

PART 1
Opener – Nerea Bermejo Olaizola, HTA Design LLP

Chapter 1
Opener – Greystar, HTA Design LLP, Tide Construction Ltd & Vision Modular Systems, Fig 1 – Office of National Statistics, redrawn by HTA Design LLP; Figs 2, 3 – Architectural Press Archive / RIBA Collections; Figs 4, 5, 6, 7 – RIBA Pix; Figs 8, 14 – Photographer: Richard Downer, Fig 9 – Photographer: Martin Charles; Fig 10, 12 – Photographer: Tim Crocker; Fig 11 – Photographer: Nick Harrison; Fig 13 – The Boundary; Figs 15, 16 – HTA Design LLP; Fig 17 – Tide Construction Ltd & Vision Modular Systems; Fig 18 – SkyVis; Figs 19, 20 – HTA Design LLP, Tide Construction Ltd & Vision Modular Systems

Chapter 2
Opener, Fig 16 – Urban Splash; Figs 1, 2, 3, 7, 14, 15 – HTA Design LLP; Figs 4, 12 – HTA Design LLP & ilke Homes; Figs 5, 6 – Rogers Stirk Harbour + Partners; Fig 8 – Photographer: Peter Cook. Design credit: TDO Architecture & George Clarke; Fig 9 – ilke Homes; Fig 10 – Keepmoat Homes; Fig 11 – Pollard Thomas Edwards & Swan NU living

Chapter 3
Opener – Photographer: Simon Kennedy. Pocket Living, Tide Construction Ltd & Vision Modular Systems; Figs 1, 2 – AHMM, Photographer: Tim Soar; Fig 3 – Richard Downer; Fig 4 – HTA Design LLP, Greystar, Tide Construction Ltd & Vision Modular Systems; Figs 5, 6, 7, 8, 9, 10, 14, 17, 21 – HTA Design LLP; Figs 11, 12, 23 – HTA Design LLP, Tide Construction Ltd & Vision Modular Systems; Fig 13 – Apex Airspace; Fig 15 – PRP; Fig 16 – Heriot Watt & HTA Design LLP; Figs 18, 19 – Waugh Thistleton; Fig 20 – Office of National Statistics, redrawn by HTA Design LLP; Fig 22 – Drink Tea Artworks/Dragages Singapore Pte Ltd

Chapter 4
Opener – HTA Design LLP, Tide Construction Ltd & Vision Modular Systems; Figs 4, 8, 9, 11, 14, 15 – HTA Design LLP; Fig 1 – T. Dasrren Nunis. Unsplash.com; Fig 2 – Mick Haupt. Unsplash.com; Fig 3 – Kirk Thornton. Unsplash.com; Fig 5 – Stan Wiechers; Fig 6 – Eames Foundation; Fig 7 – RIBA; Fig 10 – ilke Homes; Fig 12 – Pollard Thomas Edwards & Swan NU living; Fig 13 – Metropolitan Workshop; Figs 16, 17 – Photographer: Peter Cook. Design credit: TDO Architecture and George Clarke

Chapter 5
Opener – Tide Construction Ltd & Vision Modular Systems; Fig 1 – Cast Consultancy; Figs 2, 3, 5, 6 – Cast Consultancy, redrawn by HTA Design LLP; Fig 4 – Rogers Stirk Harbour + Partners; Fig 7 – Sheppard Robson; Fig 5.8 – Hufton + Crow; Fig 9 – HTA Design LLP; Fig 10; Richard Downer

Chapter 6
Opener, Fig 1 – Modscape; Fig 2 – Scandibyg; Fig 3 – Leigh & Orange Architects; Fig 4 – CWO Architects; Figs 5, 6 – Sekisui; Fig 7 – Photographer: Infinite 3D Photography; Fig 8 – Forta Pro; Fig 9 – John Lewis Marshall; Figs 10, 11 – citizenM; Fig 12 – HTA Design LLP

Chapter 7
Opener, Fig 2 – HTA Design LLP; Fig 1 – Tide Construction Ltd & Vision Modular Systems

PART 2
Opener - Nerea Bermejo Olaizola, HTA Design LLP

Case Study 1
Figs 1, 2, 3, 4, 6, 7, 8, 9, 10, 11, 12, 13, 14, 15, 16 - HTA Design LLP, Fig 5 - Tide Construction Ltd & Vision Modular Systems

Case Study 2
Figs 1, 2 - HTA Design LLP; Figs 3, 4, 5, 6, 7, 8, 9, 10, 11, 12 - Urban Splash

Case Study 3
Figs 1, 2, 3, 4, 5, 11 - HTA Design LLP; Figs 6, 7, 8, 9, 14 - Richard Downer; Figs 10, 15 - Nick Harrison; Figs 12, 13 - Billy Bolton

Case Study 4
Figs 1, 2 - HTA Design LLP; Figs 3, 4, 5, 6, 7, 8, 9, 10, 11 - Pollard Thomas Edwards & Swan NU living

Case Study 5
Figs 1, 2 - HTA Design LLP; Fig 3 - Simon Kennedy; Figs 4, 5, 6, 7, 8, 9 - Metropolitan Workshop; Fig 10 - Timothy Soar; Fig 11 - Taran Wilku; Fig 12 - Edmund Sumner

Case Study 6
Figs 1, 2, 3, 4, 5, 6 - HTA Design LLP

Case Study 7
Figs 1, 2 - HTA Design LLP, Figs 3, 4, 5, 6, 7 - Drink Tea Artworks / Dragages Singapore Pte Ltd

Case Study 8
Figs 1, 2, 3, 4, 5, 7, 9, 10, 12, 15, 16, 17, 18, 19, 20, 21, 23 - HTA Design LLP; Figs 6, 8 - Forbes Massie; Figs 11, 13 - SkyVis; Figs 14. 22 - Tide Construction Ltd & Vision Modular Systems